Īśavāsya and Māṇḍūkya Upaniṣads

Rediscovering Indian Literary Classics
(ISSN - 0972-0111)

1. *Taittirīya Upaniṣad*: With the Original Text in Sanskrit and Roman Transliteration. Translation with an Exhaustive Commentary; by Muni Narayana Prasad. (ISBN 81-246-0014-7)

2, 4-5. *Bṛhadāraṇyaka Upaniṣad*: With Original Text in Roman Transliteration. English Translation and Appendices; by Nitya Chaitanya Yati; Vol. 1: Madhu Kāṇḍa; Vol. 2: Muni Kāṇḍa; Vol. 3: Khila Kāṇḍa. (ISBN 81-246-0008-2)

3. *Kena Upaniṣad*: With the Original Text in Sanskrit and Roman Transliteration. Translation with an Extensive Commentary; by Muni Narayana Prasad. (ISBN 81-246-0034-1)

6. *Muṇḍaka Upaniṣad*: With the Original Text in Sanskrit and Roman Transliteration. Translation with an Exhaustive Commentary; by Muni Narayana Prasad. (ISBN 81-246-0105-4)

7. *Kaṭha Upaniṣad*: With the Original Text in Sanskrit and Roman transliteration. Translation with an Exhaustive Commentary; by Muni Narayana Prasad. (ISBN 81-246-0110-0)

8. *Praśna Upaniṣad*: With the Original Text in Sanskrit and Roman transliteration. Translation with an Extensive Commentary; by Muni Narayana Prasad. (ISBN 81-246-0129-1)

9. *Aitareya Upaniṣad*: With the Original Text in Sanskrit and Roman transliteration. Translation with an Extensive Commentary; by Muni Narayana Prasad. (ISBN 81-246-0142-9)

10. *Śrī Dakṣiṇāmūrti Stotram* of Śrī Śaṅkarācārya; with the commentary *Tattva Prakāśikā*; by Swami Tattvavidananda Saraswati; Edited by Puppala B. (ISBN 81-246-0210-7)

11. *Āditya Hṛdayam*: With the Commentary Tattvaprakāśikā; by Swami Tattvavidananda Saraswati (ISBN 81-246-0231-X)

12. *Vāstuśāstra*: Ancient Indian Architecture and Civil Engineering — Retrospects and Prospects; by Rahul Kumar Altekar (ISBN 81-246-0246-8)

13. *Gaṇapati Upaniṣad*: With the Commentary *Tattvaprakāśikā*; by Swami Tattvavidananda Saraswati (ISBN 81-246-0265-4)

14. *Life's Pilgrimage Through the Gītā*; by Swami Muni Narayana Prasad (ISBN 81-246-0310-3)

15. *Chāndogya Upaniṣad*; by Swami Muni Narayana Prasad (ISBN 81-246-0374-X)

Rediscovering Indian Literary Classics, no. 16

Īśavāsya and Māṇḍūkya Upaniṣads

With the original text in
Sanskrit and Roman transliteration

Translation with
an Extensive Commentary
by
Swami Muni Narayana Prasad

D.K. Printworld (P) Ltd.
New Delhi

Cataloging in Publication Data — DK
[Courtesy: D.K. Agencies (P) Ltd. <docinfo@dkagencies.com>]

Narayana Prasad, *Muni*, 1938-
Iśavāsya and Māṇḍūkya Upaniṣads : with the original text in Sanskrit and roman transliteration / translation with an extensive commentary by Swami Muni Narayana Prasad.
p. cm. — (Rediscovering Indian literary classics ; no. 16)
Text of Upanishads in Sanskrit (Devanagari and roman); translation, commentary and introductory matter in English.
Includes index.
ISBN 13: 9788124604922
ISBN 10: 8124604924

1. Upanishads. Iśopaniṣad — Commentaries 2. Upanishads. Māṇḍūkyopaniṣad — Commentaries I. Upanishads. Iśopaniṣad. English & Sanskrit. II. Upanishads. Māḍūkyopaniṣad. English & Sanskrit. III. Title. IV. Series: Rediscovering Indian literary classics ; no.16.

DDC 294.592 18 22

ISBN 13: 978-81-246-0492-2
ISBN 10: 81-246-0492-4
First published in India in 2009

Published and printed by:
D.K. Printworld (P) Ltd.
Regd. Office: 'Srikunj', F-52, Bali Nagar
Ramesh Nagar Metro Station
New Delhi-110 015
Phones: (011) 2545 3975; 2546 6019; *Fax*: (011) 2546 5926
E-mail: dkprintworld@vsnl.net
Website: www.dkprintworld.com

Preface

THESE are the last in series of Upaniṣad commentaries initiated by Narayana Gurukula, as planned by Guru Nitya Chaitanya and myself together.

Ever since Śaṅkara the great Advaitin wrote his famous commentaries on the ten major Upaniṣads, successive commentators have mostly elaborated on this ācārya's ideas. To deviate from his line of thought had come to be seen as a sort of sin for Advaitins. We, on the other hand, felt it imperative to take a fresh look at the Upaniṣads in view of all modern developments in scientific and philosophical thought. In understanding India's wisdom tradition, we had the good fortune of getting sufficient guidance from Nataraja Guru, himself a disciple of the great modern Ṛṣi Narayana Guru. Guru Nitya Chaitanya Yati took upon himself the onerous task of commenting upon the two largest Upaniṣads, *Bṛhadāraṇyaka* and *Chāndogya*. He asked me to comment on those remaining. Incidentally, he had already commented on the *Īśa* and *Māṇḍūkya Upaniṣads;* so I had only to deal with six Upaniṣads. Guru Nitya did complete the commentary on the *Bṛhadāraṇyaka* in three volumes, which was published by Messrs D.K. Preintworld. My commentaries on the six Upaniṣads were written one by one and all published by this same company. Guru's old age disabilities did not afford him the opportunity to take up work on the *Chāndogya Upaniṣad*, so I took up the task and the book has since been published.

Since Guru Nitya's commentaries on the *Īśa* and *Māṇḍūkya Upaniṣad*s were already available in print, I hesitated to write new commentaries on them. Nerertheless, I felt I had something new to say on both. Already, a commentary I had written on the *Īśa* formed part of an earlier book, *Basic Lessons on India's Wisdom*. Also, many friends of the Gurukula and the publishers themselves asked me to write commentaries on these two Upaniṣads. So I thought it best to accede.

Like commentaries on the other Upaniṣads, the Bhagavad Gītā and the works of Narayana Guru, these were written after lengthy discussions with the students and inmates of the Gurukula during our daily get together after evening prayer. And the general guidelines for these commentaries could be said to have come from my earlier days when I had the privilege to sit at the feet and attend the classes of both Nataraja Guru and Guru Nitya Chaitanya Yati. And of course, I owe a great debt to the guiding light of Narayana Guru's works.

Long time Gurukula friend Dr. Peter Oppenheimer and Mr. Ian Jaco, both from the U.S.A., took great pains to work through these texts and edit them. Their love of wisdom helped them along the way. Let all lovers of India's wisdom heritage be thankful to Messrs DK Printworld for bringing out such books as are found in the series entitled "Rediscovering Indian Literary Classics," in which they consistently keep up the highest international standard.

I offer this small volume as a altar-flower at the feet of a long line of the world's *ṛṣi*s and *guru*s that in my case reached up to Nataraja Guru and Guru Nitya Chaitanya Yati.

Varkala
21, November 2008

Swami Muni Narayana Prasad

Contents

Īśavāsya Upaniṣad

Introduction

INDIA'S culture is firmly rooted in the Vedas, the most ancient of all the world scriptures. Later cultural developments and transformations came either by promoting, revising, correcting, or even disowning these Vedas.

Originally remaining in an unsystematized form, the Vedic hymns were codified by the Ṛṣi Vyāsa into four sets, namely, *Ṛgveda, Yajurveda, Sāmaveda* and *Atharvaveda*. Each of these has in it three sections: Mantras, Brāhmaṇas and Upaniṣads. The collections of hymns (*sūktas*) praising heavenly gods (*devas*) and praying for their favours, are known as *mantras* or Saṁhitās. The Brāhmaṇas teach how burnt sacrifices are to be performed, clarifying details of all specific rites, and sometimes explaining their purpose. The Upaniṣads form the concluding portion of the Brāhmaṇas, and they deal with pure wisdom. In between the Brāhmaṇas and the Upaniṣads comes a portion known as Āraṇyakas, a sub-section of the Brāhmaṇas. As their name indicates, they are to serve as objects of meditation for those who live in forests (*araṇyas*) as *vānaprasthas* (the third stage of life as anchorites).

The rituals discussed in the Brāhmaṇas are meant to be performed by householders living in villages or towns. But on leaving home at old age and entering forests as *vānaprasthas*, the actual rituals, by necessity, would have to be replaced, and mental worship in the form of meditation would gradually become the substitute. The portion of the Vedic literature that deals with this stage is called Āraṇyakas. These could be thought of as marking the transition from Vedic ritualism to Vedāntic wisdom. The Mantras, Brāhmaṇas and Āraṇyakas together is treated as forming the *karma-kāṇḍa* (section on rituals), and the Upaniṣads the *jñāna-kāṇda* (section on wisdom).

The Upaniṣads comprise the wisdom section appended to the four Vedas. The only exception in this respect is the *Īśa Upaniṣad* which in fact forms part of the Mantra or Saṁhitā section of the *Yajurveda* as its fortieth and final chapter. It therefore is considered as marking the historical stage of transition from ritualism to wisdom and as one of the oldest Upaniṣads.

The word *upaniṣad* is comprised of two prefixes, *upa* and *ni*, followed by the verb root *ṣad*. *Upa* means, "subsidiary or the one just below"; *ni* stands for *nikaṭa*, meaning "nearby"; and *ṣad* means to "sit down." The word thus literally means, to sit down just below nearby. The texts known as the Upaniṣads try to unravel the hidden nature of the wisdom of the enlightened *gurus*, which the seekers have to receive by sitting at the feet of the *guru*, and hence the name. This imparting of wisdom implies transferring the enlightened state that a *guru* experiences within his being, into the being of the seeker–disciple. This process of wisdom transference necessarily requires an intimate bipolarity called *pārasparya* between the two. This also is implicit in the word *upaniṣad*. Many other definitions of the name also exist. Another meaning of the word is "hidden wisdom."

The lengthier of the ten major Upaniṣads are in the format of dialogues between *gurus* and disciples. Though the *Kena Upaniṣad* is also a dialogue, it does not mention the names of the *guru* and disciple; only the questions and the answers are given. Answers alone are displayed in the two shortest Upaniṣads — *Īśa* and *Māṇḍūkya* —, the questions asked being taken for granted.

All the Upaniṣads teach really one and the same wisdom — what is known as *Brahmavidyā* or *Ātmavidyā* (the Science of the Absolute or the Science of the Self). But each does it in a different way, the questions asked in each are also different. Some are in the form of a dialectical revaluation of the Vedic rituals. Such Upaniṣads give a new wisdom significance to the otherwise brute rituals. This method, instead of abnegating ritualism altogether, admits it into the fold of wisdom, while making it insignificant in the broad daylight of wisdom, as the sun does stars, and as flooding water does submerge little pools. The most glaring example of it is the *Chāndogya Upaniṣad.* The *Īśa Upaniṣad,* on the other hand, resorts to stating straightaway what *Brahmavidyā* is, bringing to relief the dialectical method, key to the hidden chambers of Vedānta. Still a touch of Vedism peeps up here and there as is natural with the Saṁhitā part of the Vedas.

Brahmavidyā popularly is known as Vedānta. Originally the word *vedānta* was a synonym for Upaniṣads, for the word means the end-part of the Vedas (*veda+anta, anta* meaning "end." The Upaniṣads generally were therefore known as Vedāntas. Only later the word, in popular usage, began to signify the philosophy of the Upaniṣads. The word *vedānta* means also, "the end of knowledge"; here the word *veda* means "knowledge." It is the end of knowledge because, knowing *Brahman* or *Ātman* as oneself marks the end of all searching for Reality, and because everything becomes known upon knowing *Brahman*. This aspect will be clarified in our comments on the *Īśa Upaniṣad.*

Though consisting of eighteen short *mantra*s (Vedic verses), five sections are distinguishable in the *Īśa Upaniṣad*. The first section, in its three *mantra*s, clarifies three different paths in human life, the former two leading to final Liberation and unconditioned Happiness, while the third leads to the demonic world of darkness and sufferings in life. The second section consisting of *mantra*s 4 and 5 portrays the contradictions one comes across when one views the absolute Reality or *Brahman* in the ordinary logical way. *Mantra*s 6 to 8 delineate the nature of the experiential awareness that transcends all such contradictions. The section from *mantra*s 9 to 14, forming the core of the Upaniṣad, explicates the *yoga-buddhi* or dialectical method of thinking that helps us transcend all dualities and the contradictions that go with them. The section formed of *mantra*s 15 to 18 is considered by the religiously minded Hindus as a prayer made by a person about to die. Really, these *mantra*s, while being in the format of a prayer to the Vedic sun-god or Pūṣan, continue the line of thought depicted in the previous section, but stress its experiential value aspect.

Śānti–Pāṭha

Peace Invocation

ॐ। पूर्णमदः पूर्णमिदं पूर्णात्पूर्णमुदच्यते।
पूर्णस्य पूर्णमादाय पूर्णमेवावशिष्यते॥
ॐ शान्तिः शान्तिः शान्तिः।

auṁ । *pūrṇam adaḥ pūrṇam idaṁ pūrṇāt pūrṇam udacyate* ।
pūrṇasya pūrṇam ādāya pūrṇam evāvaśiṣyate ॥
auṁ śāntiḥ śāntiḥ śāntiḥ ॥

That is plenitude; this is plenitude. Plenitude emanates from plenitude. On plenitude being taken from plenitude, plenitude alone remains. *Auṁ* Peace! Peace! Peace!

The text of each Upaniṣad is presented as if sandwiched between peace invocations, a form of prayer for peace in life. The origin of such a custom remains unknown as are many historical details of Indian spirituality. Still it is presumed that these are prayers recited by the students of a *gurukula,* the ancient Indian system and place of education, as they wait for the *guru* to arrive for class. The same prayer is repeated before they disperse after the class. The text of an Upaniṣad is imagined to form a class, and therefore it begins and ends with the same peace invocation.

All the Upaniṣads appended to a particular Veda share a comman *śānti-pāṭha* or peace invocation. Those tagged onto the end of the *White Yajurveda* have the present verse for their peace invocation. Philosophically this is the most profound of all such. [The *Yajurveda* has two versions: one, the *Śukla* (White) and the other the *Kr̥ṣṇa* (Black).]

Peace in life is desired by all; no one craves a life without peace. The peace generally conceived in the peace invocations is not the absolute peace resulting from *Brahman*-wisdom, but is the relative one thought of as being disturbed by three sources: one, oneself; two, others and other beings; and three, fate. Such kinds of peacelessness commonly are known as *tāpas* (sufferings) and the three together is called *tāpa-traya, traya* meaning "three." The self-caused sufferings are termed *ādhyātmika-duḥkha*s (*duḥkha* also means "suffering"), the sufferings caused by others, *ādhibhautika-duḥkha*s, and the ones caused by fate, *ādhidaivika-duḥkha*s. The avoidance and redressal of all these sufferings is always prayed for by humans as indicated by repeating the word *śāntiḥ* three times at the end of every *śānti-pāṭha.*

Pūrṇam (plenitude), in the present peace invocation refers to both "that" and "this." "That" (*adaḥ*) here signifies what ultimately exists or *Brahman,* and "this" (*idam*) signifies the world, inclusive of the knowing individual. *Brahman,* evidently and by definition is complete in itself. The world and individual entities, deriving their existence as they do from the existence of *Brahman,* are also complete in themselves, though fleeting in nature. If any insufficiency or incompleteness is noticed in these, it is only so because the perception is based on certain relative value notions of we humans. Viewed absolutely, the world is complete in its own right, and each individual being is complete in its own right.

The world, according to Vedāntic perception, is nothing other than a continuous flow of the manifest forms of the eternal and all filling Reality or *Brahman*. Though the world's existence is derived from the existence of *Brahman*, it does not become separated from *Brahman;* it rather is like an ornament-form that derives its existence from gold, or waves that derive their existence from sea-water. That means, the derived forms or creations have no existence separate from the causal substance. Such is the way the world emanates from *Brahman*, or the plenitude emanates from plenitude. For the same reason, the emanation of the world from *Brahman* does in no way affect the wholeness of *Brahman*.

The same could well be understood as related to the context of a *guru* imparting wisdom to his closest disciple, as all the Upaniṣads do. A *guru* always remains in his fullness of wisdom. A disciple, on becoming enlightened as a result of the teaching imparted to him by the *guru*, also finds his fullness of wisdom. The disciple's sense of fullness was derived from the fullness that fills the being of the *guru*. Even after imparting his fullness of wisdom to the disciple, the *guru*'s wisdom remains full and unaffected.

To say that, on plenitude being taken from plenitude, plenitude itself remains, logically speaking, is a contradiction. How can something, when fully emptied of its content, again remain full? Really, this simply is a poetically sublime way of giving expression to something ineffable. Still it is understandable mathematically. We know, zero, though of no value content, is full of meaning in all mathematical calculations. On deducting zero from zero what remains is zero itself.

Let us take another example: the triangle is a general notion in geometry. It is this generic idea of the triangle in our minds that enables us to distinguish all innumerable triangles like an *ABC, PQR, XYZ,* right angled triangle, isosceless triangle, equilateral triangle and all such, as triangles. That means, all such specific triangles derive their being from the one generic concept of the triangle. Nothing happens to the generic triangle on deriving from it any number of triangles.

To be free in all respects is the one value every human always cherishes above all else. Though other living beings also instinctively seem to like freedom, they do not apparently make deliberate and calculated efforts to ensure freedom. The absolute freedom one can expect to attain is known in India as *mukti* or *mokṣa,* and is considered the ultimate goal of human life and of all philosophizing, though it is variously named in different schools of thought. The Vedāntic wisdom expounded in the Upaniṣads also aims at *mukti,* and the means of attaining it is *jñāna* (wisdom). *Jñāna* means realizing one's inseparable oneness with the total Reality, realizing that the substance in one's own being and the substance in the being of all the worlds together, are not two. This realization renders the freedom of the total being, one's own freedom also. The freedom of the total being, being absolute, one's freedom also becomes absolute. This absolute freedom is what in Vedānta is known a *mukti* or *mokṣa.*

Now, how to actualize, in living terms, this oneness of the individual being with the total being. It is the individual seeker of Liberation who is to accomplish this. Since each individual is unique in character and temperament, one's manner of accomplishing the present goal varies from person to person. Though endlessly various, such individual temperaments could generally be classified into two: active and passive. The former type of people prefer to remain engaged in activities, while the latter like to withdraw themselves from such scenes, giving importance to knowing and let others know. But both the types long for Liberation, and each has its own way of achieving it. The active way in India is known as *pravṛtti-mārga* and the passive way *nivṛtti-mārga, pravṛtti* meaning "activities," *nivṛtti*, "withdrawal" and *mārga*, "path." How these two types of people could attain their goal is summarily dealt with in the first two *mantra*s of the *Īśa Upaniṣad,* the first dealing with the *nivṛtti-mārga,* and the second *pravṛtti-mārga*. These two spiritual means of attaining Liberation are named *jñāna-yoga* and *karma-yoga* in the *Bhagavad Gītā*. It, in verse III.3, says:

> Two paths are there in this world, O sinless one, as set forth by Me of old: the *yoga* of wisdom (*jñāna-yoga*) for men of knowledge, and the *yoga* of action (*karma-yoga*) for men of action.

Īśavāsya Upaniṣad

Verse 1

ॐ ईशावास्यमिदꣳ सर्वं
यत्किञ्च जगत्यां जगत्।
तेन त्यक्तेन भुञ्जीथा
मा गृधः कस्यस्विद्धनम्॥

auṁ īśāvāsyam idaṁ sarvaṁ
yat kiñca jagatyāṁ jagat ।
tena tyaktena buñjīthā
mā gṛdhaḥ kasyasvid dhanam ॥

All this, whatever is changeful in this world, has for its essential content, the being of the all-controlling Reality. Therefore enjoy through renouncing. Do not covet anyone's wealth. (Do not covet; whose is wealth?)

Īśa, signifying God in common parlance, is the word with which the Upaniṣad begins. Anyone familiar with the philosophy of the Upaniṣads would readily notice that the idea of a personal God, as is conceived in semitic religions, does not find favour with them. If at all the word appears in the Upaniṣads, it is in its literal sense, as the one who controls. *Īś* is the verb root, meaning "to control"; from which the word is derived. In line with the Saṁhitā part of the Vedas — that part in which this Upaniṣad appears —

it would be more appropriate to think that the word *Īśa* substitutes *Brahman* in the present Upaniṣad. The latter word, though key to all the Upaniṣads in fact, does not find place at all in this Upaniṣad.

Brahman, according to the Upaniṣads, is the one invisible substance that assumes the form of and appears as all that is visible and conceivable in all the worlds, just as gold is the invisible substance that assumes the forms of all visible ornaments. Gold, thus, is the substance that controls from within the being of all ornaments. Likewise, *Brahman* is the substance that controls the being of everything that seemingly exists, both subjectively and objectively, in all the worlds. In this sense, *Brahman* could also be considered *Īśa*. *Īśa*, thus, is the substance that pervades the being of all that is changeful constituting the world.

Gold exists eternally, but its forms are fleeting. At the same time, the two remain inseparably one. The non-duality of the two, which can neither be called gold nor ornament, is the real. Likewise, *Īśa* is the one eternal substance, and all that is changeful in the world is transient. One does not and cannot remain without the other. Without a substance no transient form can appear to be, and without an apparent form no substance does exist either. The inseparable oneness of *Īṣa* and *jagat* (world) is the real non-duality (*advaita*) visualized by the *ṛṣi* of the Upaniṣad. This non-dual reality can neither be called *Īśa* nor *jagat*.

Jagat is the word used in the Upaniṣad to denote the world. Derived from the verb root *gam*, it literally means "that which always changes." The words *jagatyām jagat* thus mean "that which is changeful in this world." These changeful forms are not merely constituted of objective physical entities; the mental world of ideas, imaginations, emotions and the like that form the subjective world also constitute the "world" as understood by Vedānta. The words *idam sarvam* (all this) indicate this. *Idam* (this) is the pronoun used in all the Upaniṣads to signify the world here and now.

How is it possible to enjoy through renouncing? The enjoyment we know is secured by possessing the thing we wish to enjoy. Renouncing something, thus, means denying ourselves the chance to enjoy it. Our concern in such enjoyments is only for our personal likes and dislikes. No thought of *Īśa* or of the other beings like us does arise there at all.

When *Īśa* is also given a place in life, our picture of life undergoes a total transformation. *Īśa* being the Reality underlying all apparent forms, ourselves included, all those forms must belong to *Īśa*. All the enjoyable objects and their enjoyers being such apparent forms, all these belong to *Īśa*. We, thus, possess nothing. We are also possessed by *Īśa*. On knowing this, we can only give up what we thought of as ours to *Īśa* and live inseparably one with *Īśa*.

Īśa's self-manifestations form the world. This world is so systematized that all the entities in it, the living as well as the non-living, exist harmoniously, one's existence ensuring the existence of the other, one's joy ensuring the joy of the other. As part of it, each individual human being also is provided with all that is needed for his or her happy existence. In short, first we renounce ourselves and our possessions to their real possessor *Īśa*, and then we enjoy what is rightful to us as part of the total system of life. This is the Upaniṣadic way of enjoying through renouncing.

Having no personal motives and desires will be natural with a person of this awareness — the awareness of oneself finding one with the whole, having no desire to possess the wealth of others being part of it.

The line *mā gṛdhaḥ kasyasvid dhanam* is interpretable in two ways. One is by putting a fullstop between *gṛdhaḥ* and *kasyasvit*. Then the line would mean, "Do not have any desire. Whose is wealth?" The answer to the question is, "All wealth is owned by *Īśa*." In the light of this, owning personal possessions is meaningless. The second interpretation is to treat the whole line as one sentence. Then it means, "Do not desire anyone's wealth."

Dhana is the word used here to denote wealth. Derived from the root *dhan*, meaning "to yield fruit," the word literally means, "that which yields the fruit of satisfaction."

Perceiving *Īśa* or *Brahman* alone in everything is the essential content of wisdom (*jñāna*). A person that follows the perception portrayed in this first *mantra* attains his or her oneness in all respects with the Total, through wisdom or *jñāna*, and hence he or she could be considered a *jñāna-yogin*.

Now we come to the alternative way of attaining oneness with the Total. This is the path of a *karma-yogin*.

Verse 2

कुर्वन्नेवेह कर्माणि
जिजीविषेच्छतꣳ समाः ।
एवं त्वयि नान्यथेतोऽस्ति
न कर्म लिप्यते नरे ॥

kurvann eveha karmāṇi
jijīviṣecchataṁ samāḥ ।

evam tvayi nānyatheto'sti
na karma lipyate nare ||

Engaged in actions here itself, one should wish to live a hundred years. If you do so, there is no way other than this by which actions do not cling to you as a human.

Desiring to live for a hundred years engaged in activities, but with no *karma* clinging to its doer, is the way suggested here for attaining Liberation. This method, as was told earlier, is meant for those who, by nature, are active in life. Liberation is not to be denied to anyone. To live a hundred years indicates the entire lifespan. The lifespan of humans traditionally is considered by Indians as one hundred years, and sometimes one hundred and twenty years.

One of the Indian religious concepts holds that the residue of the actions, whether physical, mental or verbal, one has done in life clings to one's being at a subtler level called *sūkṣma-śarīra* (subtle body) and would be carried forward to future births to suffer or enjoy their fruits. This concept would be true, if at all, only when one thinks of the actions one happens to do in life as really one's own. If such actions are not one's own, then this concept also comes to be of no value. Really this *karma*-concept is caused by ignorance (*ajñāna*). How so?

Each one of us has the capability to do physical works, to do mental works and also to communicate with others using words. Did we create these capabilities? No, these are part of our being as willed and planned by nature (*prakṛti*). The word *prakṛti* itself means, "that which is constantly active." That means, with no action (*kṛti*) taking place, nature will no longer be nature; with no '*kṛti*' there would be no word *'prakṛti'* either. The entire *prakṛti* is always active. Being part of it, we also remain helplessly active. Then, when we do something, is it really we individuals who do the actions, or is it *prakṛti* that does them? Closely looked at, it is clear that we individuals really have no *karma* of our own. It is *prakṛti* or nature that acts. We, in our ignorance, think the actions that occur through us are ours. Making this point tellingly clear, the *Bhagavad Gītā* says:

> *prakṛteḥ kriyamāṇāni*
> *guṇaiḥ karmāṇi sarvaśaḥ* ।
> *ahaṁkāra-vimūḍhātmā*
> *kartāham iti manyate* ॥ — III.27

> Actions in every way take place because of the *guṇas* of *prakṛti*. Deluded by I-sense, one holds, "I am the doer."

The *Gītā* clarifies that when we, as individuals, consider ourselves as doers of actions (*kartās*), we are mistaken. If at all *karmas* have a doer, it is *prakṛti*, because all actions take place in *prakṛti* or nature.

Now what is *prakṛti*? It is nothing but the absolute Reality existing in a creatively self-unfolding state. Really, that Reality cannot and does not remain otherwise. Thus it could well be said, all the *karmas* take place in that Reality, also called *Ātman* or *Brahman*. Narayana Guru, in the *Karma Darśanam* of his *Darśanamālā* (Garland of Visions) categorically says,

> *ātmaiva māyayā karma*
> *karoti bahurūpadhṛk* ।
> *asaṅgaḥ svaprakāśo'pi*
> *nidrayām iva taijasaḥ* ॥ — VI.1

> *Ātmā* alone, while being completely unattached to anything and self-luminosity in essence, performs all the *karmas* by assuming various forms by virtue of its own *māyā*. It is like *taijasa* (dreaming) while asleep.

This *karma*-power in *Ātmā* finds expression universally as the wind blowing, water flowing, fire burning, the earth supporting everything and the like, and individually as the heart beating, blood circulating, gases inside making sounds, lungs breathing, digestive system functioning, hands working, mind thinking, words being uttered and the like. All these clearly show how individuals really have no *karma* of their own. They imagine that they have *karmas* simply because they think and willfully desire to do certain actions with certain ends in view. All such willings are merely functions of the mind, and the mind was so devised not by us but by nature. The willful desiring of minds is thus also the *karma* of *prakṛti*. In short, an individual thinking, revolving about the idea that he has his own *karmas*, happens because of his lack of understanding of life. This ignorance in Vedānta is known as *ajñāna*.

Karmas cling to individuals only if such are done by them. If done by *prakṛti*, not by them, then they become free of all *karmas* as residues, and realize that *karmas* clinging to them is merely superimposed on them simply because of *ajñāna*. Narayana Guru, therefore at the close of his *Brahmavidyā Pañcakam* (The Science of the Absolute in Five Verses) says,

> *prārabdham kvanu sañcitam tava kim āgāmi kva karmāpy asat* ||5 ||
> How could there be for you
> Then the bondage of *karmas*,
> Whether already begun *(prārabdha)*,

> Accumulated from the past (*sañcita*)
> Or those yet to be accumulated (*āgāmī*)?
> *Karma* is itself unreal.

On attaining the transparency of vision just made clear, they remain liberated even when being engaged in activities natural to them and necessitated to do as part of the overall flow of nature. This should be the sense in which the present *mantra* says, *na karma lipyate nare* (actions do not cling to you as a human).

Performing actions with this enlightenment transforms all actions into a sort of *yajña;* that is to say, each action becomes an oblation offered into the fire of *Ātman* or *Brahman.* Actions otherwise performed cause bondage called *karma-bandha,* the feeling that one is bound by the actions one does. The *Bhagavad Gītā* therefore says again,

> *yajñārthāt karmano'nyatra*
> *loko'yam karma-bandhanaḥ* ।
> *tad artham karma kaunteya*
> *mukta-sangaḥ sam ācara* ॥ — III.9

> People become bound by actions, unless performed as *yajña.* Therefore, O Arjuna, do actions properly free from attachments, in the sense of *yajña*s.

Treating actions in this manner requires a proper understanding of life. That means, one can remain a *karma-yogin* only if endowed with wisdom, only if one is a *jñānin* or a *jñāna-yogin.* A *jñāna-yogin,* in the world of here and now, can remain only as a *karma-yogin,* because no *jñānin* can exist without *karma,* physical, mental or verbal. Therefore, this second *mantra* could be treated also as a continuation of the first, clarifying how a *jñāna-yogin* actually lives in this world. Then the second half of the *mantra* could be treated as showing how such a *jñānin* lives fully liberated with no *karma* clinging to him.

And now we come to the case of those who remain in the darkness of ignorance.

Verse 3

असुर्या नाम ते लोका
अन्धेन तमसाऽऽवृताः ।
ताꣳस्ते प्रेत्याभिगच्छन्ति
ये के चात्महनो जनाः ॥

asuryā nāma te lokā
andhena tamasā 'vṛtāḥ ।
tāṁste pretyābhigacchanti
ye ke cātmahano janāḥ ॥

Demonic, indeed, are those worlds overcovered by blinding darkness. To those worlds go those who are the killers of the self, having departed.

This *mantra* states what happens to those who are the killers of the self (*ātma-hano janāḥ*). Who are they? Not knowing the self or oneself, and living a life in complete ignorance of oneself, in Vedāntic terms, is equal to one having killed oneself. The killers of the self mentioned here, thus, are such.

They, according to this *mantra*, reach the demonic world (*asuryā nāma lokāḥ*). *Asuras*, according to Vedism and Indian mythology, are the enemies of the gods (*devas* or *suras*), and they (*asuras*) inhabit the underworld. *Deva* means "one who is brightness in essence," and *sura* (the opposite of *asura*), "one who gives in plenty" (*suṣṭum rāti iti surah*).

Because humans constantly ask for favours from the gods, we can see the idea behind this name *sura.*

There is no human being in whom desires find a definite end. A new desire arises in the mind once another is fulfilled, or when another disappointedly remains unfulfilled. This goes on endlessly. Therefore, the real satisfaction of having all one's desires completely fulfilled finds a place only within those who absolutely have no desires. Such people feel that all the gods' favours have been received. This nature becomes well rooted in them because of the brightness (*deva*) of proper wisdom. Therefore such are termed as of *daivī-sampatti* (divine character) in the *Bhagavad Gītā*. The whole of its chapter XVI is set aside to differentiate the *daivī-sampatti* and *āsurī-sampatti* (demonic qualities) of man. In other words, though the Vedas and mythological legends think of a world inhabited by *asura*s (demons), the real *asura*s live in our own inner world, making us suffer ceaselessly from our own unfulfilled desires. A detailed description of the demonic qualities in humans is given in the *Gītā*. Part of it reads as follows:

idam adya mayā labdham
imam prāpsye manoradham ।
idam astīdam api me
bhaviṣyati punar dhanam ॥

asau mayā hataḥ śatrur
haniṣye cāparān api ।
īśvaro 'ham aham bhogī
siddho 'ham balavān sukhī ॥

āḍhyo 'bhijanavān asmi
ko 'nyo 'sti sadṛśo mayā ।

yakṣye dāsyāmi modiṣya
ity ajñāna-vimohitāḥ ||

aneka-citta-vibhrāntā
moha-jāla-samāvṛtāḥ |
praṣaktāḥ kāma-bhogeṣu
patanti narake 'śucau || — XVI. 13-16

This much I could gain today. The other wish I'll fulfil shortly. This much wealth do I possess now, and much more will be mine before long.

That enemy has been slain by me; the others will also be done away with by me. I am the ruler. I do enjoy everything. I satisfy my ambitions. I am powerful. I am happy.

I am rich and high-born. Who is there equal to me? I will perform fire-sacrifices; I will give gifts; I will enjoy life. Deluded thus by ignorance are they.

Involved in many things at a time, they make themselves confused and mad. They get entangled in the meshes of delusion. Addicted to lustful gratifications, they fall into hellish foulness.

The indication is that those who do not know themselves virtually kill themselves by living in the blinding darkness of ignorance. They, in effect, make their own lives a world of *asuras* or demons.

The word *pretya* could be translated as "on departing from this world on death," but in this philosophical context it would be more appropriate to take it as denoting "having departed from the world of the Real." The religiously minded, taking the word *pretya* in the former sense, may treat the *mantra* as meaning thus:

> Demonic indeed are those worlds overcovered by blinding darkness. To those worlds go those who suicide on departing from this world.

Though literally interpretable so, the sense is not of any wisdom significance, and does not show any continuity with the ideas of the two previous *mantras*. Of course, the moral message it gives is not to be ignored.

The next two *mantras* concentrate on the contradictions we come across when the one non-dual Reality is tried to be understood logically.

Verse 4

अनेजदेकं मनसो जवीयो
नैनद्देवा आप्नुवन् पूर्वमर्षत् ।
तद्धावतोऽन्यानत्येति तिष्ठत्
तस्मिन्नपो मातरिश्वा दधाति ॥

anejad ekaṁ manaso javīyo
nainad devā āpnuvan pūrvam arṣat ।
tad dhāvato 'nyān atyeti tiṣṭhat
tasminn apo mātariśvā dadhāti ॥

> Unmoving, the One is swifter than mind. The shining ones (senses) do not reach It because It is ever ahead of them. It, standing still, outstrips those who run. Within Its being, the all-pervading vital airs support the activities of beings.

The contradictory statements made here about *Ātmā* or *Īśa* are only apparently so, when seen with a logically, mechanistically biased mind. *Īśa* is neither a mechanistic nor a logically conceivable system of existence. It is the absolute Reality from which all the mechanistic systems are devised by the human mind, out of what already exists undeniably. Hence that Reality always remains out of reach for such methods of thinking. How can the source of logical thinking be known through the very same logic?

Although appearing contradictory, all that is stated here would be found coherent when seen by a person who intuitively perceives *Īśa* in his own being, as the *ṛṣi* who uttered these words did.

To say that something does not move, and that it is swifter than mind, is contradictory. So is the statememt that something standing still can, at the same time, outstrip all others. But all such statements could be seen as fully consistent with the non-relative, non-dual status of *Īśa* or *Ātmā*.

Being the one Substance that fills the being of everything, subjectively and objectively, grossly and subtly, *Īśa* does not have a place to move to. In that sense *Īśa* is unmoving.

Modern Science has established that there is nothing faster than light in the physical universe; therefore the speed of light is termed absolute velocity. Light travels 3,00,000 Km per second. At this speed, light takes many many years to reach from one star to another or its orbiting planet. But mind takes virtually no time to reach such stars or planets. Mind, thus, is faster than light. This mind takes at least the duration of a blink to reach a star. On reaching there, the mind finds that *Īśa* is already there as the Substance in the being of the star. *Īśa*, thus, is faster than the mind in flight.

The Substance that underlies the being of everything in all the worlds, in number, has undoubtedly and necessarily to be one.

The shining ones (*devas*) mentioned here refer to the senses, for it is their shining that enables them to perceive objects. The word *devas*, though is the Vedic and mythological contexts are taken to represent the inhabitants of heaven, in the philosophical context it stands for the senses, when scrutinizing the literal sense — the shining ones — of the word. And for this reason the word *devas* is widely in use in the Upaniṣads to denote the senses.

The sense organs have their corresponding objects — ears have sound for their object, skin has touch, eyes have forms, tongue has taste and nose has smell. *Īśa*, the all-underlying Substance, is no object of the sense organs. Besides, *Īśa* is the one source of both the sense organs and their objects. Since *Īśa* is the Substance that underlies the being of both the sense organs and their objects, how can the very sense organs make *Īśa* their objects of perception? Perceiving anything with our sense organs, in the usual course of knowing, is what we are familiar with; often such perceptions are considered the basis of all other kinds of knowledge such as inference. Being so, on hearing of *Īśa*, we may first think of perceiving It or He by making use of our sense organs. But it is impossible. The more we try to catch *Īśa* with our sense organs the more we feel It or He is running far ahead of us.

Īśa is not only the one Substance in all kinds of beings in all the worlds, It also is what energizes all these beings into life, and in this sense is called *prāṇa*. The senses and their objects also thus derive their vitality from *Īśa*. Such vital energies could be thought of as having two dimensions: the universal and the individual. Universally, the entire universe is to be conceived as a living entity, known in modern philosophy as Gaia. The vitalizing principle in it is termed here *mātariśvā* meaning "air." Every individual being, whether organic or inorganic, also has functioning in it a life principle of its own. This, in the inorganic world, is indicated by the phenomenon, for example, of crystallization of salt. Such vitalities functioning in a living being are thought of as five in number by Indian philosophers: *prāṇa, apāna, vyāna, udāna,* and *samāna.* All these five are considered to have a universal facet as well. All such being the functions of vital air, it is said here, "Within Its being the all-pervading vital airs support the activities of beings."

The next *mantra* continues portraying how logically contradictory the *Īśa* appears to be.

Verse 5

तदेजति तन्नैजति
तद्दूरे तद्वन्तिके ।
तदन्तरस्य सर्वस्य
तदु सर्वस्यास्य बाह्यतः ॥५॥

tad ejati tan naijati
tad dūre tadvantike ।
tad antarasya sarvasya
tad u sarvasyāsya bāhyataḥ ॥

It moves, and It moves not. It is far away, and It is very near. It is within everything here, and It is outside everything here.

Every context of knowing involves a knowing mind and an object to be known. The context of knowing *Īśa* might also be thought of as such. Really *Īśa* is no object of knowledge. As far as a knower is concerned, *Īśa* can be realized only as the Substance of his/her own being. One, therefore, does not have to seek *Īśa* as an object; one has only to look at oneself with an interiorized eye. Unless guided by an enlightened *guru*, one would either remain completely oblivious of the existence of *Īśa*, or if at all one happens to become aware of the existence of *Īśa*, would search for Him/It as an object of knowledge as everything else.

In the case of those who remain in complete ignorance of *Īśa*'s existence, unless they by chance turn and become inquisitive of the life's meaning and other such fundamental questions, they can only be ignored. Those who are already in search of *Īśa*, on the other hand, need proper guidance, or else they become lost when facing logical contradictions. The first question such seekers would ask upon meeting a *guru* would be how to resolve such paradoxes inevitably faced when thinking of *Īśa*. The *guru* tells them not only how such contradictions are plausible in logical thinking, but how *Īśa* transcends all of them also.

Īśa being the one Substance that appears as everything in all the worlds, He/It can never be known as an object of knowledge other than as His/Its manifest forms. Any search for *Īśa*, therefore, as an object external to the knower would be futile. The more one tries to know *Īśa* so, the more He/It is felt to be moving (*ejati*) unreachably further away (*dūre*).

All the manifest forms of *Īśa*, that constitute the world, are in a state of motion, known as the eternal flux. In that sense, *Īśa* moves constantly. But, being the all-filling Substance, with nowhere else existing to move to, *Īśa* is motionless. Seen as the Substance in the knower's own being also, He/It is not felt to be moving at all, because no one feels oneself to be moving away from oneself. Oneself or the Substance in one's being is the nearest to oneself. Therefore an interiorized perception makes *Īśa* known as the nearest to oneself (*antike*).

Īśa is the only Reality that exists and manifests as everything. What appears as inside and outside, therefore, is the same *Īśa*. "Inside" and "outside" really are relative terms. From the point of view of one manifest form, all other manifest forms are external. What appears as "inside" and "outside" to each manifest form is the same *Īśa*. Thus *Īśa* is both inside and outside everything.

The next two *mantra*s concentrate on the experiential awareness of the one *Īśa* that is beyond all such contradictions.

Verse 6

यस्तु सर्वाणि भूतानि
आत्मन्येवानुपश्यति ।
सर्वभूतेषु चात्मानं
ततो न विजुगुप्सते ॥

yastu sarvāṇi bhūtāni
ātmany evānupaśyati ।
sarva-bhūteṣu cātmānaṁ
tato na vijugupsate ॥

> He who perceives all beings in the Self or in himself and the Self or himself in all beings at the same time, he for this reason feels no disgust for any being.

He who perceives the non-duality of the one and the many, finds nothing as other than himself, and thus feels no disgust towards anything.

Many are the apparent forms, whereas one is the all-underlying Substance or *Īśa. Īśa,* in this *mantra* is replaced by *Ātmā* or the Self. The word *ātmā* is derived from the verb root *āt* meaning "to pervade" (*ād-vyāpane*). Thus the substance that pervades the being of something is its *ātmā.* Gold, thus, is the *ātmā* of an ornament; water is the *ātmā,* generically of the ocean, and specifically of its waves. Ornament forms are many, while their gold substance is one; waves are many while their water-content is one. Likewise, all beings in all worlds have *Ātmā* for their underlying Substance. The same Substance is also known as *Brahman* in the sense that It grows always as everything. The word *brahman* is derived from the root *bṛh,* meaning "to grow" (*bṛhi vṛddhau*).

Suppose an ornament seeks to know, "Who am I?" The proper answer would be, "I am Gold." Similarly, "I am water" will be the correct self-knowledge of a wave. Then the ornament feels, "I, being gold, am in all the ornaments, and the existence of all the ornament forms is in me, the gold." A wave, likewise, feels, "Because I am water, I am in all the waves, and the existence of all the waves is in me, the water." Similarly, an individual being, on realizing "I am *Ātmā,*" perceives itself/the Self in all the beings, and the existence of all the beings in itself/the Self. The words "Self" and "oneself" thus become synonymous, and in Sanskrit, the same word *ātmā* is used to denote both.

The original word in the text for "beings" is *bhūtāni,* the plural of the word *bhūta* which means "that which has come into being." *Bhūta* is a word derived from the verb root *bhū* meaning, "to become," "to exist" (*bhū sattāyām*). *Bhūta,* thus, means "that which appears to be as an existing entity" (*bhāva*). All the apparent entities, living as well as non-living, constitute the *bhāva*s, and the Substance that assumes these *bhāva*s is *Ātmā*. Metaphysically, *Ātmā,* in the *Bhagavad Gītā,* is called *sat* (that which is ultimately Real), and all its manifest forms, *bhāva*s. If ornament forms are *bhāva*s, gold is the *sat*. Without appearing in some transient manifest forms (*bhāva*s) like that of ornaments, the eternal gold-substance cannot and does not exist anywhere, and without gold existing, no ornament form can appear to be either. One's existence is impossible and meaningless without the other. Really, the two never exist separately; their separateness being only ideas in our mind. Even when we conceive of the two as two, they actually remain inseparably one. The same is true with the relation between the appearance of the *bhūta*s or the world and *Ātmā*. The *Bhagavad Gītā* emphatically says.

nāsato vidyate bhāvo
nābhāvo vidyate sataḥ ।
ubhayor api dṛṣṭo 'ntas-
tv-anayos tattvadarśibhiḥ ॥ — II.16

> The unreal cannot manifest itself; the Real never exists without manifesting itself. The inherent truth of these two has thus been perceived by the seers of ultimate Reality.

Such a one who perceives the inseparable oneness of the two or their non-duality, has nothing to detest, because everything, whether or not relatively counted as good or evil, is a manifest form of the one non-dual *Ātmā*. Without such manifest forms, and other than as such manifest forms, *Ātmā* does not exist.

Sat is one and *bhāva*s are many. The one and the many thus becoming inseparably one, the eternal and the transient thus becoming inseparably one, logically viewed, again, is a paradox. One who intuitively and experientially perceives their oneness through the dialectical approach, as explicated in *mantras* 9 to 14 to follow, finds nothing to detest for the simple reason that one does not detest oneself.

It is often accused that Vedānta does not teach people to love fellow beings, as some religions do, for example Christianity. This is true only literally. What Vedānta does is try to lift humans to the highest realm of wisdom by realizing one's identity with every being. Realizing this goal results not only in hating no being as stated in the present *mantra,* but instead in necessarily and spontaneously loving each being. Though no positive instruction to love is made by the Upaniṣads, the enlightenment effected by them makes man naturally an enbodiment of love.

Verse 7

यस्मिन् सर्वाणि भूतानि
आत्मैवाभूद्विजानतः।
तत्र को मोहः कः शोकः
एकत्वमनुपश्यतः॥

yasmin sarvāṇi bhūtāni
ātmaivābhūd vijānataḥ ।
tatra ko mohaḥ kaḥ śokaḥ
ekatvam anupaśyataḥ ॥

To the one who is well aware that all beings have indeed become oneself/the Self, to the one who thus perceives oneness constantly, what delusion is there, what sorrow is there?

Uncontrollable, unceasing sorrows are what very often make people think of the life's meaning and similar fundamental problems. This thinking ultimatly takes them, if inquisitive enough, to the experience of oneness portrayed in *mantra* 6. All world religions also try in their own way to free man of all his afflictions in life. All philosophizing too, particularly in the East, is aimed at this very same goal.

What ultimately is the cause of sorrows? Delusion (*moha*) is its real cause. Delusion is one's confused state of mind as to what is real and what is unreal. Removing this delusion and enabling one to perceive clearly and directly what really exists comprises the essence of wisdom.

This essence of wisdom was made clear in the previous *mantra*, and the same is restated here with a different tone — that of inwardly experiencing all beings and the entire world as being in oneself. What appears as the world is the constantly changing manifest forms of *Ātmā*, the real content in oneself. This process of self-unfoldment of *Ātmā*, that happens because of the infinite creative urge inherent in *Ātmā*, finds expression as everything, both pleasant and unpleasant, both good and evil, both *dharma* (righteousness) and *adharma* (unrighteousness). Perceiving all that happens in life and the world as part of *Ātmā*'s sportive self-unfoldment, and thus as not different from what is ultimately Real, enables one to treat both happiness and suffering with a state of equanimity, and thus both pleasure and pain as equals. This brings in a sense of peacefulness that renders life a constant flow of unconditioned Happiness (*paramānanda*). The duality of happiness and suffering pertains to the relative or conditioned realm of existence alone. The intuitive awareness of the oneness of *Ātmā* and the world, releases us from this realm of relativism and leads us to Absolutism, where pleasure and pain would be treated as equals. All the dualities we perceive in life are caused by our ignorance about ourselves or *Ātmā*, called *ajñāna*, referred to here as delusion (*moha*).

This oneness is not just to be perceived at a particular time, say while in meditation, but is to be experienced all through one's life, at every moment. Everything that happens in life, including our own deliberate attempt to manipulate such events, merely is a minute element in the one *Ātmā*'s self-unfoldment, as is suggested by the word *anupaśyataḥ* (to the one who inwardly perceives constantly). It is such a constant experience of oneness that frees us of all sufferings.

The next *mantra* portrays the experiential nature of *Ātmā*, and how the infinite potential for the world's unfoldment along with its entire structural perfection, is inherent in *Ātmā*.

Verse 8

स पर्यगाच्छुक्रमकायमव्रणम-
स्नाविरꣳशुद्धमपापविद्धम् ।
कविर्मनीषी परिभूः स्वयंभू-
र्याथातथ्यतोऽर्थान् व्यदधाच्छाश्वतीभ्यः समाभ्यः ॥

sa paryagac chukram akāyam avr̥aṇam
asnāviraṁ śuddham apāpa-viddham ।
kavir manīṣī paribhūḥ svayaṁbhūr yāthāta-
thyato 'rthān vyadadhāc chāśvatībhyaḥ samābhyaḥ ॥

He is all-pervading; He is pure radiance; He is bodiless; He is invulnerable; He is sinewless; He is pure; He is untainted by sin; He is the all-wise, the one of proper understanding, the one that becomes everything everywhere, and He is self-existent. He assigns throughout endless years various objects according to their natures (as His self-unfoldment).

Īśa, referred to in the first *mantra* and later perceived as *Ātmā*, is the one Substance, *sat-cit-ānanda* (Existence-Consciousness-Value-sense) in essence, that unfolds Itself/Himself as everything. In that sense He/It is all-pervading (*paryagāt*).

Being the unconditioned Substance that is Consciousness (*cit*) in essence, It/He is radiant or is pure radiance, for Consciousness is never experienced other than as pure effulgence (*śukram*).

It has appearances that have forms. Reality as such is formless, as gold is formless and thus invisible, while all its apparent forms like ornaments have forms and thus are visible. *Ātmā*, similarly, while appearing as everything that has form, Itself is formless or bodiless (*akāyam*).

Vraṇa means "wound." That which has a body alone can be wounded. A bodiless entity never becomes subject to any wound. All that is apparent, in all the worlds, is subject to being wounded, but the Substance that assumes these forms is never wounded. A wound caused to a form simply results in the appearance of a new facet of the Substance, causing no substantial change to It. It thus is invulnerable (*avraṇa*).

Sinews, tissues, muscles and all such form part of the physical body of an animal, humans included, as one of the countless kinds of forms in which the one Reality appears. The bodiless Reality or *Ātmā* underlying them therefore, has no sinew, no tissue, no muscle and thus is *asnāviram* (sinewless).

Being conditioned by nothing, *Ātmā* is pure (*śuddham*).

Sin (*pāpa*) and merit (*puṇya*) are concepts created by

man about his own activities based on certain value notions. Such activities, really are forms in which the inherent creative urge in *Ātmā* finds self-expression. The value notion that differentiates sin and merit are also conceived by the human mind, mainly with man's likes and dislikes and certain social conventions for their bases. The one Substance (*sat*) that unfolds Itself as all human activities, the one Consciousness (*cit*) that unfolds Itself as all ideas and notions, the one Value-sense (*ānanda*) that unfolds Itself as all value-concepts, is beyond the duality of sin and merit, and thus is untainted by sin (*apāpa-viddham*). The human mind, conditioned as it is, is always tainted by sin, but the Consciousness that unfolds Itself as the human mind is not subject to any sin.

Consciousness in essence, *Ātmā* is conscious of all that happens within Itself, and nothing other than as what happens within *Ātmā* exists anywhere or any time. Thus *Ātmā* is *kavi,* meaning "the one who knows everything, one who is wise in all respects." The word *kavi* commonly is used to denote a poet. A poet gives expression to what he imaginatively perceives within himself. The same happens within *Ātmā* as It creates the world from within Itself.

The word *manīṣin* could be interpreted in two ways: Firstly, one who cogitates (*manana*) on things properly and perceives life accordingly, and secondly, one who is in full control (*īśa*) of the mind (*manas*). *Ātmā*'s cogitation on what are the things to be unfolded from Itself is proper in Its own way, of course a way not comprehensible to the human mind, and *Ātmā* is in full control of Its own imaginations (*saṁkalpa*), the main function of mind (*manas*). Thus in both senses, *Ātmā* is a *manīṣin*.

Ātmā being the Reality that manifests Itself as all the worlds, It is *pari-bhūḥ*, *pari* meaning "everywhere" or "all around," and *bhūḥ*, "that which becomes," and it is rendered here as "that which becomes everything everywhere."

The question, "How did this originate?" is commonly asked in the course of any scientifically-minded enquiry. This question is inanswerable in regard to the one source of everything, because attempting to do so leads to the fallacy of infinite regression. That means, the question of how everything originated is answered by saying *Ātmā* or *Īśa* is the material-cum-efficient cause of everything. The question how was *Īśa* (God) originated takes us infinitely backwards into asking again and again, "How was that causal Reality originated?" at each stage of enquiry. This kind of enquiry is pointless. Therefore, one final cause, *Īśa* or *Ātmā*, is thought of as causeless, and thus self-originated and self-existent, both implied by the word *svayambhūḥ*.

The world that emanates from *Ātmā* or *Īśa* is not a chaos. It is so perfect in its structural coherence that no one can tamper with it, though the existence of the world is in a constant state of change. The world having a structural coherence means, all such possibilities are inherent in the causal Substance or *Ātmā*. The changefulness of the world causes the sense of the time-flow, and all that happens throughout that flow is nothing other than *Ātmā* finding Its self-expression. Therefore it is said, "He assigns throughout endless years various objects according to their nature (*yāthātathyato 'rthān, vyadadhāc chāśvatībhyaḥ samābhyaḥ*)."

Now we pass on to the heart of the Upaniṣad, where

the dialectical secret implied in transcending inevitable paradoxes and attaining Immortality is unravelled.

Verse 9

अन्धं तमः प्रविशन्ति
येऽविद्यामुपासते ।
ततो भूय इव ते तमो
य उ विद्यायाꣳ रताः ॥

andhaṁ tamaḥ praviśanti
ye 'vidyām upāsate ।
tato bhūya iva te tamo
ya u vidyāyṁ̐ ratāḥ ॥

Into a blinding darkness enter those who adore ignorance (*avidyā*), and more pitch-black, as it were, is the darkness entered by those who delight in knowledge (*vidyā*).

Apparently paradoxical is the statement this *mantra* contains.

Vidyā-avidyā (knowledge-ignorance, to be more precise, science-nescience) and *sambhūti-vināśa* (creative becoming-destruction), along with *amṛtam-mṛtyuḥ* (immortality-death) are the dualities the present set of six *mantra*s try to transcend. The *mantra*s make use of these three sets of dualities belonging to three different epistemological contexts, in order to enable the contemplatively-minded seeker to delve into the depths of the dialectical methodology, known in India as *yoga-buddhi*. Many of the world scriptures rely on this methodology to help seekers realize the ultimate Reality that is not amenable to ordinary logical thinking.

Let us first see what *vidyā* and *avidyā* are. A clear definition of these two core terms of Vedānta seems not forthcoming in any of the scriptures or even in the introductory textbooks on Vedānta and traditional commentaries. Narayana Guru defines the two terms as follows:

> *anātmā na sad ātmā sad*
> *iti vidyotate yayā* ।
> *sā vidyeyam yathā rajju-*
> *sarpa-tattvāvadhāraṇam* ॥
>
> That because of which the non-Self (*anātmā*) is understood as unreal, and the Self (*Ātmā*) as Real, is what this *vidyā* is, as in the case of ascertaining that the snake is unreal and the rope alone is real.
>
> *ātmā na sad anātmā sad*
> *iti vidyotate yayā* ।
> *saivāvidyā yathā rajju-*
> *sarpayor ayathārtha-dṛk* ॥
>
> That because of which the Self (*Ātmā*) is understood as unreal and the non-Self (*anātmā*) as real, is what this *avidyā* is, as in the case of wrongly seeing the rope as unreal and the snake as real. — *Darśanamālā* IV.3-4

The state of awareness in which the unreal is mistaken for the Real is known as *ajñāna* (ignorance). And the function of consciousness because of which this *ajñāna* happens is called *avidyā*. *Ajñāna* and *avidyā* thus are words different in connotation. That *Ātmā* or *Īśa* is what ultimately exists has already become clear in the very first *mantra* itself and also that the world-appearance has no real existence of its own and thus is unreal.

The one in ignorance, instead of taking life and the world as part of the self-unfoldment of *Ātmā*, *sat-cit-ānanda* in essence, will perceive it as the ocean of sufferings. Sufferings really are merely part of life. As day is followed by night, as an incline is followed by a decline, happiness is followed by sufferings. Such is the cyclic nature that *Ātmā*'s unfoldment is structured. The question, "Why is it so?" does not arise. The miseries of some may happen to be worse than those of others. The sense of responsibility in man, another facet of the manifestation of the *cit* aspect of *Ātmā*, demands that those who have share with the have-nots; those who suffer more are consoled and helped by those who are of less sufferings. Treating life as an ocean of sufferings itself makes it difficult for us to face problems with a sense of equanimity. On the other hand, having the proper understanding of life makes it easier to face difficulties with a balanced state of mind.

A life without sufferings should never be expected. Yet we simply forget that sufferings form part of life also. Such is the dark world we are pushed into because of a lack of understanding life (*ajñāna*) caused by *avidyā*.

More pitch-black, it is said, is the state of those who delight in *vidyā*. It is to brightness, not to darkness, that the *vidyā* we are familiar with, and according to the above given definition, leads us to. *Vidyā* enables us to understand that *Ātmā* alone is Real, and that *anātmā* is unreal. All that appears and disappears forms *anātmā*. Understanding can never be an experience of darkness. But this understanding as well as the *vidyā* that causes it, is not something to be delighted on. Proper understanding or *vidyā* leads us to experience our own mergence into the being of *Ātmā* or *Īśa* where no enjoyer-enjoyed duality is relevant. A person of such awareness never thinks, "I am a man of wisdom" or

"I am delighted on being a *jñānin.*" As long as one enjoys *vidyā,* one's enjoyerhood or I-sense (*ahaṁkāra*) predominates. That state of mind distances one from the real spirit of wisdom.

It would sometimes be possible to save one caught in *avidyā* by proper guidance. But the case of one who enjoys *vidyā* is different. Being a person proud of having gained wisdom, being proud by considering himself a *jñānin,* he can never be saved from the darkness he is in. That darkness, thus, is more pitch-black.

Verse 10

अन्यदेवाहुर्विद्यया
अन्यदाहुरविद्यया ।
इति शुश्रुम धीराणां
ये नस्तद्विचचक्षिरे ॥

anyad evāhur vidyayā
anyād āhur avidyayā ।
iti śuśruma dhīrāṇāṁ
ye nas tad vicacakṣire ॥

Distinct, indeed, it is said, is the outcome of knowledge (*vidyā*), and distinct the outcome of ignorance (*avidyā*). We have heard thus from the wise ones who have explicated these to us.

The outcome of *vidyā,* as was already stated, is attainig wisdom (*jñāna*) and of *avidyā, ajñāna.* Those in the state of *ajñāna* do not think of the real and do not discriminate between the real and the unreal. As a result, they consider what they perceive with their senses as real, and the pleasure these give as what makes life meaningful. Faced with sufferings, faced with problems in life, they feel totally lost, sometimes cursing themselves and even God.

Those in ignorance think of life as beginning with birth and ending with death. The problem of what happens after death worries them. The fear that the fruits of their actions (*karmas*) in this life will have to be eaten in the next life ever torments them. Death is the most frightful event as far as they are concerned. In short, having to suffer and fearfully feeling destined to die are the end-results of *avidyā*.

The outcome of *vidyā*, on the other hand, is different. It ensures us wisdom (*jñāna*). And this *jñāna* enables us to ignore the fleeting appearances in life, including pains and pleasures. A *jñānin* does not treat sufferings as something miserable, but as one of the constantly altering facets of the everlasting process of life. He thus faces life's sufferings and ill-fated events also with a well balanced state of mind, enabling him to face them boldly.

A *jñānin* considers death also not as a frightful event marking the termination of life, to be detested, but as an inevitable facet of the onward process of life. Death, in his view, is simply the opposite pole of birth. If Reality is comparable to an ocean that exists eternally, individual beings, then, are like waves that arise from and merge back into the ocean. The emerging of a wave, then, is the event that we call birth, and its merging back, death. Really an individual wave has no existence of its own apart from the ocean. Likewise, an individual has no existence of his/her own apart from *Ātmā*, and thus is unreal. Considering the birth and death of what is unreal certainly is meaningless.

Birth is considered a joyous event and death a frightening, detestable one when these events pertain to our close friends and relatives. How many births and deaths take place in the world every second, not only among humans, but among living beings as a whole? Do these events make us concerned? No. These events affect us, not because they are births and deaths, but because they happen to those dear to us. That means, it is in the realm of relativism that birth and death are of concern for us; in the absolutist sense, both events are considered, even by *ajñānins,* as forming part of the overall system of life. Then, why not consider the births and deaths of our dear ones also so?

Jñāna makes us realize, "I really am *Ātmā* or *Īśa* in essential content. My individuated form is just a fleeting appearance. It disappears. I, the *Ātmā,* do not disappear, and really I was never born. I am really immortal." In short, immortality is the ultimate outcome of *jñāna,* whereas its opposite, death, is the result of remaining an *ajñānin.*

Discriminating these two realms of knowledge is in itself considered one of the essential prerequisites of a true seeker of wisdom or *jñāna.* This ability to discriminate, often known as *viveka,* or to be more precise, *nitya-anitya-vastu-viveka* (ability to discriminate the eternal reality from transient appearances), does not imply realizing the essential content of wisdom. *Viveka* just means one's ability to think that something exists eternally underlying all that appears and disappears. The search for that one Substance eventually leads to Self-Realization, that is to say, realizing, "I am that one eternal Reality in essence." This realization is known as *ātma-jñāna* (self-knowledge), which in essence is realizing one's own immortality. Discrimination thus marks both the beginning and the end of the search for wisdom. The discrimination that one eternal Reality must exist, in contradistinction to all transient appearances, marks the beginning of all spiritual enquiry. But the finality of attaining wisdom is marked by the discriminative awareness that *Ātmā* alone is what eternally exists, and what appears as the world of fleeting forms called *anātmā* (non-self), is but momentary manifestations arising in the very same *Ātmā.*

This discrimination has always been extolled by the wise from time immemorial. Such wise ones are known as seers or *ṛṣi*s. *Dhīraḥ* is the word used here to denote such a wise one. The word means, "one who offers wisdom" (*dhiyam rāti iti dhīraḥ*). One who possesses something alone can offer it. Thus, one who possess wisdom and offers it to those who seek, is to be counted as a *dhīraḥ.*

Verse 11

विद्यां चाविद्यां च
यस्तद्वेदोभयꣳ सह ।
अविद्यया मृत्युं तीर्त्वा
विद्ययाऽमृतमश्नुते ॥

vidyāṁ cāvidyāṁ ca
yas tad vedobhayam̐ saha ।
avidyayā mṛtyuṁ tīrtvā
vidyayā 'mṛtam aśnute ॥

Knowledge and ignorance (science and nescience) — he who understands these two together, crosses death through ignorance (nescience) and enjoys immortality through knowledge (science).

We have already seen what *vidyā* and *avidyā* are. Both are knowledges, the former the right way of knowing and the latter the wrong way of knowing. Both are functional modes of consciosness (*cit*), the essential content of *Ātmā*. Resultnig in a wrong understanding of life, *avidyā* could be treated as the negative mode of the knownig function of consciousness, and *vidyā* as its positive mode. This bifurcation would not have happened had consciousness remained functionless. But it never remains so because of the creative urge for self-unfoldment, called *māyā*, inherent in it. It could thus well be said, it is because of *māyā* that the non-dual Consciousness (*cit*) appears functionally as the *vidyā-avidyā* duality. Narayana Guru makes this point clear in his *Ātmopadeśa Śatakam* (One Hundred Verses of Self-Instruction) thus:

> Seen from one side, there are various activities;
> They seem to be real because of nescience (*avidyā*).
> Seen from the other, there is perceived
> pure and unconditioned Consciousness alone,
> And this is what constitutes
> The realm of true knowledge (*vidyā*).
> It is *māyā* that makes the real
> appear always thus as two-sided.
> The enlightened awakening that transcends this duality
> Alone assures the *turīya* state. — verse 72

The most glaring evidence of this methodology of transcending the duality, as adopted in the *Bhagavad Gītā*, is the verse II.16 already quoted in our comments on *mantra* 6 above.

The effect of *avidyā* is that of making us think of ourselves as the doers of actions, and also as having birth and death. *Avidyā*, in a sense, is what brings in death (*mṛtyuḥ*). Frightened of death, we feel the necessity of overcoming it one way or another.

Avidyā is a negative functional mode of consciousness; death, its effect, has a negative value in ordinary life and hence is to be avoided; avoiding something is a negative process. Thus, everything related to *avidyā* is of a negative nature.

Vidyā, on the other hand, effects our enlightenment that we may become *jñānins*. *Vidyā* is a positive mode of expression of the knowing function of consciousness. This enlightenment liberates us from the sense of being mortal and enables us to realize our immortality as *Ātmā.* The ultimate effect of *vidyā,* thus, makes us immortal. *Vidyā* is a positive facet of the function of consciousness; its value is a positive one, being something aspirable; immortality (*amr̥tam*) and enjoying it (*aśnute*) is a positive effort.

Getting rid of *avidyā* and resorting to *vidyā* mean the same; to avoid death and to enjoy immortality mean the same. Of all these pairs, one side is negative and the other is positive. The final goal is neither positive nor negative; it is something neutral that exists between the two: the two are the extreme poles of manifest forms, just as a magnet remains neutral in between its south and north poles.

We think of ourselves as dying simply because of our *avidyā,* and having an understanding of this fact, that is, by knownig the *avidyā* principle, we overcome death, its effect. That means, we would then feel, "My thinking that I was destined to die was merely because of *avidyā;* now I am free of that."

Similarly, *vidyā* is the function of consciousness that enables us to attain *jñāna* and thus immortality. That means, through *vidyā* we attain immortality.

Just as it is *māyā* that causes the dual appearance of *vidyā* and *avidyā* in the *cit* (Consciousness) content of *Ātmā,* it is the same *māyā* that causes the dual appearance of death and immortality in the *ānanda* (Value sense) content of *Ātmā*. Just as *vidyā* and *avidyā* find non-dual oneness in Consciousness (*cit*), death and immortality find the same non-dual oneness in the *ānanda* content of *Ātmā*.

Ātmā never remains inactive without the phenomenal appearance of birth and death. Consciousness never remains inactive without appearing as *vidyā* and *avidhyā*. Without assuming the forms of death and immortality, causing extreme suffering and extreme happiness, the *ānanda* content of *Ātmā* never remains inactive. Attaining the non-dual oneness of all these like that of the gold-substance and ornament-forms, has to be the final goal of any Vedāntic search for Reality.

Put otherwise, *vidyā* and *avidyā* are two explicable counterparts of a dialectical situation involving an inexplicable and ineffable Reality. The one Consciousness-Reality transcends this duality. Death (*mr̥tyuḥ*) and immortality (*amr̥tam*) are similar opposite poles of yet another dialectical situation. What is really to be attained transcends these dualities, and it is left unmentioned simply because it is beyond the bounds of verbal expression. *Vidyā-avidyā*, overcoming-enjoying, *mr̥tyuḥ-amr̥tam* are all dual concepts that enable a contemplative seeker to visualize intuitively within, the non-dual Reality or Goal. Such is the way the present Upaniṣad openly uses the dialetical methodology to transcend dualities. Similar dualities are mind-matter, internal-external, subject-object, cause-effect, gross-subtle, body-soul and the like.

All the other Upaniṣads and all the world-scriptures as well could be seen tacitly relying on this method of expounding the ineffable. The *Bhagavad Gītā* claims itself to be a *yoga-śāstra* (the science of dialectics) because it makes use of this method throughout its text to expound the Vedāntic wisdom. Dialectics, in a sense, is a master-key that helps us open the inner chambers of all the world-scriptures. It is a science of *yoga* in the sense that it joins together (*yuj*) two opposite poles of a situation. *Yuj* is the verb root from which the word *yoga* is derived, which means, "that which joins together the two."

The *vidyā-avidyā* duality pertains to the realm of the knowing function of consciousness (*cit*). Another aspect, besides *cit* and *ānanda*, of *Ātmā* is that of *sat* (Existence). In that realm also we encounter the same kind of duality, again related to *ānanda* or death and immortality. In the place of *vidyā-avidyā*, the dual facets we come across here are that of creative becoming (*saṁbhūti*) and destruction (*vināśa* or *asaṁbhūti*). The nature of this duality-realm, and how it is transcended contemplatively by making use of this dialectical method, is shown is the next three *mantras*.

Verse 12

अन्धं तमः प्रविशन्ति
येऽसंभूतिमुपासते ।
ततो भूय इव ते तमो
य उ संभूत्याꣳ रताः ॥

andhaṁ tamaḥ praviśanti
ye 'saṁbhūtim upāsate ।
tato bhūya iva te tamo
ya u saṁbhūtyāṁ̐ ratāḥ ॥

Into blinding darkness enter those who adore non-becoming (*asaṁbhūti*), and more pitch black, as it were, is the darkness entered by those who delight in creative becoming (*saṁbhūti*).

Asaṁbhūti or *vināśa* (non-becoming or destruction) and *saṁbhūti* (creative becoming) mark the beginning and end of the phenomenal existence of individual entities, as well as the world. Those who consider phenomenal appearances as real treat the destruction or rather the dissolution of their own individuated existence as marking the end of life. They live in worry about death. Contemplating on death, as though adoring it, would be normal with them. Some even live fearful of the end of the world itself as some charlatans prophecy. Such people sometimes even prepare themselves to face the end of the world, forgetful that such preparations are meaningless in the context of total annihilation. They live completely oblivious of what life is. They are ignorant that what we call death or destruction is simply a stage of transfiguration of what really exists, and that what really exists never ceases to exist. Those who thus meditate on death or destruction all through life, as if it were a frightful event, live constantly in a dark world of blinding ignorance.

Saṁbhūti, the opposite pole of *asaṁbhūti*, means creative becoming; birth is the corresponding pole of death; the creation of the world is the corresponding pole of its own dissolution. If the death of an individual and the dissolution of the world are considered fearsome, the birth of an individual, and the creation of the world, are taken as joyous events. To be more philosophical, the opposite pole of death is immortality, and attaining it somehow is always dreamt by ordinary people as the best of all attainments in life. They thus think that attaining a state without death, if at all possible, is the happiest of all events. They simply forget, at least for the time being, of the natural ageing process, the disabilities and pains of old age and life's miserable condition at too old an age. They remain also oblivious to the fact that the incessant cyclic process of birth and death is what ensures the ever new and immortal existence of life.

Those who treat the birth of an individual being, the creation of the world, or attaining the state of deathlessness as joyous, live in a darkness more blinding than those who are fearful of death. At least those who live worried over death can turn more easily toward thinking of the real meaning of life and what really exists, than those who are joyous.

Attaining immortality could also be considered in its philosophical sense. Such an immortality is not something to be delighted on. Those who treat it so and make efforts in life to attain that happiest of all events, live in a world more blinding than do the ignorant. In the real Immortality, no enjoying, no enjoyer and no enjoyed remain to be reckoned because all these merge into the one, all engulfing effulgence of enlightenment.

Verse 13

अन्यदेवाहुः सम्भवाद्
अन्यदाहुरसम्भवात् ।
इति शुश्रुम धीराणां
ये नस्तद्विचचक्षिरे ॥

anyad evāhuḥ sambhavād
anyad āhur asambhavāt ।
iti śuśruma dhīrāṇāṁ
ye nas tad vicacakṣire ॥

Distinct, indeed, it is said, is the outcome of creative becoming (*sambhava*), and distinct the outcome of non-becoming (*asambhava*). We have heard thus from the wise ones who have explicated these to us.

There are those who concentrate on the *saṁbhūti* or the *sambhava* aspect of life. They find that life is meant for merry making, looking as they are, always at the positive aspects of life. They naturally remain optimistic. What they ultimately can aspire for is to attain immortality, which they also might treat as an object of pleasure.

There are also those who direct their interest and attention toward the *asaṁbhūti* or *asambhava* aspects of life. They perceive life as full of sufferings and remain pessimistic. They always remain alert to the negative aspects of life. Death being treated as the most terrific event in life, they always remain fearful of death. Such people are often considered by the Upaniṣads as virtually already dead, though biologically living.

Saṁbhūti and *asaṁbhūti* (referred to as *vināśa* — destruction — in the next *mantra*) are thus diametrically opposite in nature, as are their outcomes.

Verse 14

सम्भूतिं च विनाशं च
यस्तद्वेदोभयꣳ सह।
विनाशेन मृत्युं तीर्त्वा
सम्भूत्याऽमृतमश्नुते॥

sambhūtiṁ ca vināśaṁ ca
yas tad vedobhayam̐ saha ।
vināśena mṛtyuṁ tīrtvā
sambhūtyā 'mṛtam aśnute ॥

Creative becoming (*saṁbhūti*) and destruction (*vināśa*) — he who understands these two together, crosses death through destruction and attains immortality through creative becoming.

Saṁbhūti forms the positive extreme of life and *vināśa* the negative extreme. *Saṁbhūti* makes us happy and *vināśa* unhappy. Birth is the most conspicuous aspect of *saṁbhūti* and death that of *vināśa.* These two really are part of the rolling on of the wheel of *prakṛti* or nature. One who is capable of understanding these two as dialectical counterparts of the eternal progression of life, is to be considered a *yogī*. What a *yogī* experiences throughout his life is of having attained the ultimate goal of life. Is this goal overcoming death or attaining immortality? It is neither or both; it is simply the non-dual, ineffable inner transparence and peace which could neither be counted as crossing death nor as attaining immortality. Both birth and death would be treated equally by such a person of attainment.

Death is fearful only because of one's ignorance about the destruction-aspect (*vināśa*) that forms part of the eternal unfoldment of life in the *Ātmā* that alone exists. Becoming enlightened of this truth liberates one from the fear of death and virtually from death itself. This is the way one crosses over death through *vināśa.*

Birth also, likewise, forms the opposite side of the death aspect of life, and the exhileration we feel of it is also so. Such is how the *saṁbhūti* aspect of life affects each of us. The most sublime of all *saṁbhūti* in life is that of attaining immortality. One's enlightenment of this *saṁbhūti* aspect thus leads one to immortality.

Really "crossing death" and "attaining immortality" denote the same inner event, the former a statement made upon observing it from its negative side, and the latter from the positive side. Suppose one is asked, "Do you want to overcome death, or to attain immortality?" The natural answer will be, "Both, as I see, mean the same." But what is this one meaning of the two statements diametrically opposite in nature, one totally negative and the other totally positive?

Death is a phenomenon negative in value, detested by all humans; *avidyā* and *asambhūti* or *vināśa* that make one think of death as frightful are of negative nature; and avoiding is a negative effort. On the other hand, immortality is of a positive value aspired by all; *vidyā* and *saṁbhūti* causal to attaining it are of positive nature and attaining is a positive effort. One statement, thus, is negative in all respects, and the other positive in all respects. Yet both mean the same. This neutral meaning content really is not verbally expressible. We can simply make statements about it looking at from its one side or the other. Neither of the apparent sides is real, just as neither of the two sides of a coin is real; but what exists in between the two sides is the real. Likewise, the neutral meaning bracketed by these two opposite statements is what the seeker is really expected to seek and realize.

What is really meant to be conveyed, thus, is not clearly expressed in these words of the Upaniṣad. Being ineffable, it is left to the seeker to meditatively visualize on his own. Such is the subtle dialectical methodology adopted in the present Upaniṣad. In the other Upaniṣads also, the same method could be seen explicitly or implicitly resorted to in a manner that fully agrees with the relevant context dealt with.

Yet another aspect of dialectics that hides at the core here also needs to be disclosed. The *vidyā-avidyā* duality pertains to the realm of knowing, one of the functions of the *cit* (conciousness) aspect of *Ātmā*. The *saṁbhūti-vināśa* duality, on the other hand, comes within the context of the manifestation of what really exists, that means to the *sat* (Existence) aspect of *Ātmā.* If the former context, in mathematical terminology, could be considered similar to the vertical axis or *Y*-axis in a graph, then the latter belongs to the horizontal axis or *X*-axis of the same. Then, *vidyā* could be placed at the positive pole of the vertical axis and *avidyā* at its negative pole. Similarly, *saṁbhūti* could be seen as pertaining to the plus pole and *asaṁbhūti* to the minus pole of the harizontal axis. Then the neutral point marked by "*O*" is neither vertical nor horizontal, neither plus nor minus. Finding oneself at this neutral point is what we call the experience of *paramānanda* (*parama,* supreme; *ānanda,* Value experience or Happiness). Realizing this marks the final attainment Vedānta aims at, the state in which one feels, "I don't want to know anything more." This could be graphically represented as follows:

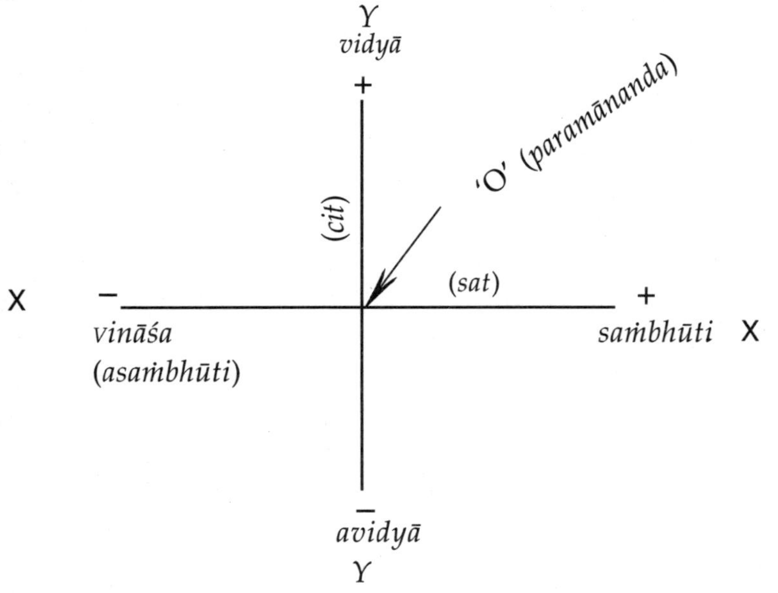

Verse 15

हिरण्मयेन पात्रेण
सत्यस्यापिहितं मुखम् ।
तत्त्वं पूषन्नपावृणु
सत्यधर्माय दृष्टये ॥

hiraṇmayena pātreṇa
satyasyāpihitaṁ mukhaṁ ।
tat tvam puṣann apāvṛṇu
satyadharmāya dṛṣṭaye ॥

The face of Reality is covered over with a golden casket. Uncover it, O Pūṣan, so that I who puts the Real to practice in life, may behold it.

The first thing we notice in this *mantra* is that, it, leaving behind the Vedāntic concepts of *Īśa* and *Ātmā,* relies on *pūṣā,* the Sun-God of Vedism. This conceptual tilt does justice to Vedism proper, to which context, technically speaking, this Upaniṣad belongs. Still, it is of wisdom significance. The word *pūṣā,* though the name of a Vedic god, literally means "the one who nourishes," and is derived from the verb root *puṣ*, meaning "to nourish" (*puṣa puṣṭau*). *Īśa* or *Ātmā,* we know, is the Reality that nourishes every being by systematizing a cosmic life-scheme in which every living being ensures the existence and nourishment of other beings. The present drift from Vedāntic terminology to the Vedic one, could be seen to continue through the rest of the Upaniṣad. Perhaps because of this change in tone, this last section of the Upaniṣad, consisting of *mantra*s 15 to 18, is often considered by the religiously minded as forming a prayer made by a person about to die.

The Upaniṣad has so far been trying to develop systematically a line of thought by which the core teaching of *Brahma-vidyā* (the science of the Absolute) could be revealed. And the way of giving expression to the inexpressible, by resorting to the dialectical method or *yoga-buddhi*, has just been delineated. In short, the Upaniṣad has made clear, in a very concise way, what is to be revealed and how is it to be revealed.

This Upaniṣad, we should notice, is an attempt to lead the seeker gently to the experiential enlightenment of the inexpressible by making use of the expressible word. Put differently, the limitations of words that cannot directly express what ultimately exists, are themselves employed to overcome the words themselves. The Upaniṣadic *ṛṣi*, therfore, after accomplishing all that is verbally possible, virtually tells the seeker:

> If you think what I have just said reveals what you expect to realize, you are wrong. What I have shown you through these words is simply the golden casket in which what you really seek is hidden. The words I have uttered may sound very attractive and meaningful just like a golden casket. Therefore you may mistake the casket for the priceless treasure you are in search of. Don't be misled. Be prepared, in your mind, to open this golden-casket-like-words of mine and perceive directly the unsaid Reality preserved within.

Those who remain satisfied with the golden appearance of the casket may not even think of the gem kept within. The existence of such a hidden gem has to be brought to their notice by a real living *guru* who has already perceived it. Coming in contact with such a *guru* in life happens only by chance or by God's grace, or the grace of the very *Ātmā* or *Īśa* they are in search of, for such an event is in no one's control. Therefore, that Reality, conceived here as *pūṣa*, is entreated to be gracious enough to open this casket and enable one to perceive the Real Secret of the Upaniṣadic teaching. It is here that the meaning "secret teaching" of the word *upaniṣad* becomes fully significant.

The one who utters the prayer here qualifies himself as *satya-dharma,* rendered here as, "one who puts the real to practice in life." *Satya* means "the Truth, the Real," and is something to be grasped and realized as an internally experienced enlightenment. When this enlightenment guides the actual day-to-day life, it is called *dharma* or righteousness. *Satya-dharma* thus means a person who realizes the Real or *Ātmā* and also lives his life as the external expression of that enlightenment. The theoretical *satya* and practical *dharma* become inseparably one, one validating the other.

According to the traditional way in which this *mantra* is interpreted, the golden casket that overcovers the Real is the veiling power (*āvaraṇa-śakti*) of *māyā.* Uncovering this *māyā*-veil enables the *satya-dharma* to perceive the Real without hindrance, that will then guide his life by that wisdom.

The next *mantra* reveals how the one for whom the golden casket has become open, inwardly perceives what is within.

Verse 16

पूषन्नेकर्षे यम सूर्य प्राजापत्य
व्यूह रश्मीन समूह ।
तेजो यत्ते रूपं कल्याणतमं तत्ते पश्यामि
योऽसावसौ पुरुषः सोऽहमस्मि ॥

pūṣann ekerṣe yama sūrya prājāpatya
vyūha raśmīn samūha ।

tejo yat te rūpaṁ
kalyāṇa-tamaṁ tat te paśyāmi
yo 'sāvasau puruṣaḥ so 'ham asmi ॥

O Nourisher (*pūṣan*), O the sole seer (*ekarṣi*), O the one who curbs (*yama*), O Sun (*sūrya*), O the one related to Prajāpati, gather back a portion of your splendid rays so that I may behold the brilliant, auspicious form of yours. (The unseen universal) person (*puruṣa*) that I behold (in you) — I am He.

Īśa or *Ātmā* is addressed here with various epithets; all these pertain to Vedism. *Pūṣan*, we know, means "the one who nourishes." *Ṛṣi* means a seer, the seer of the ultimate Reality, the one who perceives clearly how the one Reality exists creatively. Really, the Reality is itself the seer of how it exists creatively because no other reality exists to see how it exists. *Ātmā,* thus is the one seer (*ekarṣi*) of itself and the beholder of all that happens in itself.

Yama means "one who curbs and controls everything so that things do not go chaotic in nature." Nature retains its immutable structural perfection in spite of the changeful nature of everything that constitutes it, because *Ātmā,* the all-underlying Substance, is in full control of everything. This becomes possible because *Ātmā* is Consciousness in essence.

Sūrya (sun) means literally, "the one who is always on the move." *Ātmā* also, in its apparent form of the world, is in a constant state of flow called the eternal flux. In this sense, *Ātmā* could be thought of as a sort of *sūrya,* like the ordinary sun (Sūrya) that moves around illumining the entire world.

Prajāpati, according to Vedism, is the god or principle that presides over creation; and *prājāpatya* is the one who or that which is related to Prajāpati, or the one related to the context of creation. *Ātmā* alone, being the Reality that has existence, is Itself the god that presides over the creation of everything from Itself, and thus *Ātmā* is *prājāpatya.*

Yama being also the name of the god of death, that reference suggests destruction; *sūrya* indicates the cyclic nature of whatever exists; and *prājāpatya* the creation. These three words, thus, suggest *Ātmā* as the cause of dissolution, sustenance and creation respectively of the world.

That *Ātmā* is pure effulgence we have already noticed. Just as the blazing midday sun cannot be directly looked at, *Ātmā*'s effulgence-content is too bright to be looked at or conceived. Hence the prayer made by the supplicant for the partial withholding of its brilliance that he may directly look upon it.

Ātmā, being *ānanda* in essence, could also be seen as the beautiful, since beauty (*rūpa* or *saundarya*) is *ānanda* (happiness) perceived. The context here being that of perceiving the sun, Happiness is rightly altered as beauty, signified by the word *rūpa* which also means "form." The beautiful, auspicious and brilliant form of *Ātmā*, when seen directly, is perceived by the supplicant as himself, because what is real in the universal aspect of the self-manifestation of *Ātmā* is itself what is real in the individuated aspect of the same also. If the universal being of the world could be compared to a city (*pura*), then the one who resides in that city, the inner content of its being is the *puruṣa* (person). *Puruṣa* is defined as, "the one who reposes in the city (*pura*)" (*pure śete iti puruṣaḥ*). The same is the *puruṣa* that reposes in the little city of the individual being also. Therefore the supplicant says "*so'ham*" (*saḥ+aham*), meaning "I am He."

This is one of those sayings quite familiar in the world of Indian spirituality. It is a variant version of the *mahā-vākya* (great dictum) *aham brahma asmi* (I am *Brahman*) of Vedānta.

Verse 17

वायुरनिलममृतमथेदं
भस्मान्तꣳ शरीरम् ।
ॐ क्रतो स्मर कृतꣳ स्मर
क्रतो स्मर कृतꣳ स्मर ॥

vāyur anilam amṛtam athedaṁ
bhasmāntaṁ śarīraṁ ।
auṁ krato smara kṛtam̐ smara
kṛato smara kṛtam̐ smara ॥

The vital air (*vāyu*) becomes the immortal air (*anila*); and then this perishable body turns into ashes. O mind, remember *auṁ*. Remember what you have done. O mind, remember. Remember (the world constituted of actions) that was made.

The last *mantra,* with its references to *yama, sūrya* and *prājāpatya,* made us think of the dissolution, sustenance and creation, respectively, of the world. Of these three phenomena pertaining to the appearance of the world and individual beings, it is dissolution or death that often makes people pensive and worrisome.

What really is death? We have already seen how existence has universal and individuated facets. Death is nothing but an individuated apparent form losing its identity as an individual and becoming merged with the universal. It is an event just like a drop of water merging into the ocean. No destruction of what really exists really takes place at the event of death or at the dissolution of the world.

This merger takes place both at the subtle and gross levels of existence. At the subtle level, the vital air, usually called *prāṇa,* but here referred to as *vāyu,* meaning "air," becomes merged in the universal immortal air termed here (*anilam amṛtam*). Likewise, the physical gross body becomes merged with earth, thus turning into dust or ashes; if buried the body directly becomes dust, and if cremated it becomes part of the soil in a different way, leaving some ashes behind, which also go nowhere other than into the soil. In short, what we call death is an event that makes what is mortal in our being merge into the immortal (*amṛtam*) being, and therefore it is not an event to be mourned. One's own mind is asked here to remember this truth. It, in principle, is equal to remembering *auṁ*.

The mind is asked also to remember all that it has done in life (*kṛtam*). How is this to be remembered as directed here? By remembering the (*kṛtam*) or that which has been made or created. That means, by remembering the world that was created. What is special about it? Its emergence was, or rather is, the result of the creative action (*kṛtam*) of *Ātmā* and the world thus created (*kṛtam*) is also virtually a flow of *karma*s. It never remains actionless at any point of its existence. The mind is asked to remember that the actions performed by it are nothing more than part of the immortal self-activation of *Ātmā.* This rememberance enables the individual to attain immortality within the realm of the mind also, as were the *prāṇa*'s and the body's attainment of immortality portrayed earlier.

The thought that one has one's own *karma*s makes one

feel bound to them, whereas seeing all *karma*s as part of the immortal *karma* of *Ātmā* liberates one from all *karma*-related bondages whilst engaged in life's normal activities. Such an awareness can also deter one from performing any action motivated by mere wilful personal motives that go aganist the overall flow of *Ātmā*'s self-expression. It is when the personal will and the unpredictable will of *Ātmā,* in respect of *karma*s, do fully agree with each other, that one's actions are truly morally sound. In other words, the above said awareness also serves as a formidable moral force in life.

Verse 18

अग्ने नय सुपथा राये
अस्मान् विश्वानि देव वयुनानि विद्वान् ।
युयोध्यस्मज्जुहुराणमेनो
भूयिष्ठां ते नम उक्तिं विधेम ॥

agne naya supathā rāye
asmān viśvāni deva vāyunāni vidvān ।
yuyodhy asmaj juhurāṇam eno
bhūyiṣṭhāṁ te nama uktiṁ vidhema ॥

O fire, lead us along the auspicious path to the goal of Supreme Felicity, O God who knows the secret of all actions. Take away from us all the deceitful faults. We offer our best salutations to you!

Ātmā, again in line with the Vedic tradition, is addressed here as Agni, the Fire-God. In the ritualistic context of Vedism, Agni is the god who conveys all oblations offered by humans into the gods in heaven, who are meant to be pleased by the fire-sacrifices. Being brightness in essence, it, in the wisdom context, could stand for *Ātmā,* in all respects. *Ātmā* is often compared to a bonfire, of which every individual entity that emerges and disappears, is a spark. The entire world, then, is an aggregate of such momentary sparks. Such sparks never cease to emerge from *Ātmā* either. How this *Ātmā* is the knower of all *karma*s happening within itself has already been discussed.

The auspicious path (*supatha*) is the one to immortality so far being chalked out. Treading along it requires a courageous resoluteness and wilfulness, qualities one acquires only as nature-given or God-given. The only God being *Ātmā,* imagining it as fire, it is entreated to lead the supplicant to his proper goal. All that stands aganist this spiritual progress in life is summarily designated as "faults" (*enas*) here, which could also be translated as "sin." And with this heartfelt prayer, the Upaniṣad comes to a close.

शान्तिपाठः

(Śāntipāṭhaḥ)

ॐ पूर्णमदः पूर्णमिदं
पूर्णात् पूर्णमुदच्यते ।
पूर्णस्य पूर्णमादाय
पूर्णमेवावशिष्यते ॥
ॐ शान्तिः शान्तिः शान्तिः ॥

auṁ pūrṇam adaḥ pūrṇam idaṁ
pūrṇāt pūrṇam udacyate ।
pūrṇasya pūrṇam ādāya
pūrṇam evāvaśiṣyate ॥
auṁ śāntiḥ śāntiḥ śāntiḥ ॥

That is plenitude; this is plenitude. Plenitude emanates from plenitude. One plenitude being taken of plenitude, Plenitude alone remains. *Auṁ* peace! peace! peace!

Māṇḍūkya Upaniṣad

Introduction

AUṀ, in the context of Indian spirituality, is the most sacred of all words. It is accepted so both by the ritualistic Vedism and by the wisdom-teaching Vedānta. *Auṁ*, in the ritualistic context, is the sound with which permission is given, by the chief brāhmaṇa, priest to begin an actual fire ceremony. Recitation of all the Vedic *mantra*s is started by pronouncing *auṁ* (*oṁ*) in order to show that doing so has the proper permission of the chief priest. *Auṁ* then is known as *anujñākṣara* (permission-giving-syllable). In the wisdom context, on the other hand, the same word serves as the verbal symbol connoting the ultimate Reality or *Brahman*. Known also as *praṇava*, literally that which is ever new, *auṁ* is cited in the *Yoga-sūtras* of Patañjali as the word (*vācaka*) denoting God. The concerned *sūtra* reads, "*tasya vācakaḥ praṇavaḥ*" (1.27) which means "*praṇava* is the word that denotes Him." ("Him" here stands for God [*Iśvara*] mentioned in the *sūtra* just before.) Trying to explicate how this monosyllable condenses within itself *Brahman* or *Ātman*, the one Substance in all the worlds, is what the present Upaniṣad does.

This Upaniṣad's name *Māṇḍūkya* derives probably from the name of the Ṛṣi Maṇḍūka who visualized it. It reveals how the monosyllable *auṁ* acquired this unique and all-inclusive wisdom significance. Appended to the

Atharvaveda (the other three of the four Vedas are *Ṛg*, *Yajur* and *Sāma*), it is also the shortest Upaniṣad, the longest being *Bṛhadāraṇyaka* that follows the tradition of *Yajurveda*. Upaniṣads are texts that contain the basic wisdom teachings that emerged as a sort of revaluation of the brute Vedic ritualism.

The number of such Upaniṣads, as traditionally held, is 1008. But no one knows which and what these are. The number of available Upaniṣads, as collated and published by Messrs. Motilal Banarasidass, Delhi in a single volume, is 188. Some of the texts included in this volume are not worth counting as Upaniṣads. A reasonable tradition holds that there are 108 Upaniṣads, probably because "108" is treated as a holy number in India. Still, which are these 108 Upaniṣads is a question yet to be settled.

The most authentic proponent of Advaita Vedānta, Śaṅkara, wrote commentaries on the major ten of these Upaniṣads. These ten are named in a single verse as follows:

> *īśa-kena-kaṭha-praśna muṇḍa-māṇḍūkya-tittirī* ।
> *aitareyam ca chāndogyam bṛhadāraṇyakam ucyate* ॥

> The ten Upaniṣads (called *daśopaniṣads*), thus are, *Īśa, Kena, Kaṭha, Praśna, Muṇḍaka, Māṇḍūkya, Taittirīya, Aitareya, Chāndogya* and *Bṛhadāraṇyaka*.

A knowledge of all these Upaniṣads is recommended for those who take to the path of wisdom in life. Even though Śaṅkara wrote commentaries on the *prasthāna-traya* (the three basic texts of Vedānta consisting of the Upaniṣads, *Brahma-Sūtras* of Bādarāyaṇa, and *Bhagavad Gītā*) within a short span of his life, becoming fully acquainted with the wisdom content of these basic textbooks of Vedānta requires more than a life time of contemplative studies, something quite impossible for most. Those who find it too difficult, then, are recommended to study the ten Upaniṣads alone of the *prasthāna-traya,* along with their commentaries. If even that is found too much, it is suggested to keenly study the *Māṇḍūkya Upaniṣad* alone. Such is the importance given to this shortest of all Upaniṣads, perhaps because it unravels the wisdom significance of the most sacred syllable *auṁ.*

Underscoring the high position in spirituality gained by this monosyllable, the *Kaṭha Upaniṣad* says,

> *sarve vedā yat padam āmananti*
> *tapāṁsi sarvāṇi ca yad vadanti* ।
> *yad icchanto brahmacaryam caranti*
> *tat te padam saṁgraheṇa bravīmi oṁ ity etat* ॥
> — I.1.15

> [*Yama said:*] The word which all the Vedas declare, which all the austere enquiries proclaim (as their goal), aimed at which *brahmacarya* is practised in life — that word I shall tell you in a nutshell: It is *Aum.*

To attain a transparent vision of what *Auṁ* or *praṇava* really signifies is thought to mark the state of enlightenment. Of this state, the *Bhagavad Gītā* says:

> *yaj jñātvā neha bhūyo 'nyat*
> *jñātavyam avaśiṣyate.* — VII.2

> . . . on knowing which, nothing remains yet to be known.

Such is the great task taken up by this Upaniṣad, and for that matter by the present student of the Upaniṣad.

****

Auṁ is a word. It also has a meaning as every other word does. All ordinary words in each language signify something specific, either perceivable or conceivable. Many are the objects that exist externally, and each such is denoted by a word. What is perceivable or conceivable, in this context, in Vedānta, is referred to as *rūpa,* meaning "form"; and the word that signifies it is *nāma* or "name." The world, therefore, is thought to consist of names and forms *(nāma-rūpātmaka).*

A mango tree stands in front of my room. It is of the variety known as Malgova. Many such Malgova mango trees grow in our garden, each having its own peculiar shape and growth pattern. A "Malgova mango tree" is here generic in significance related to each specific Malgova mango tree. If "mango tree" is thought of as generic, then "Malgova mango tree" is specific; it becomes included within what is understood by "mango tree." Mango tree, similarly becomes specific in significance when we think of "trees" generally, because the word "tree" includes within its meaning all kinds of trees. Like this, the scope of generic concepts could be expanded to end with a term that excludes nothing in all the worlds, perceivable or conceivable, from what it signifies. That word is *auṁ* according to Vedāntic semantics.

My idea of the particular Malgova mongo tree in front of me is very distinct, whereas what is meant by "Malgova mango tree" generally is not so distinct. At the same time, the meaning of the words "Malgova mango tree" is distinct when compared to what is denoted by the words "mango tree," which is still more vague. Still more indistinct is the term "tree." That means, the more generic the meaning of a term becomes, the more indistinct its meaning becomes.

Then, what the most generic of all terms, i.e., *auṁ*, denotes has necessarily to be the most indistinct of all meanings. So indistinct and generic is the *Brahman* or *Ātman* that the word *auṁ* denotes. How this most indistinct meaning of the word *auṁ* could be understood, at least intuitively, is the basic problem the Ṛṣi Maṇḍūka tackcles in the present Upaniṣad.

Everything in the world is represented in the world of language by a word. The perceivable and conceivable entities are endless in number; so are the words that signify them. This Upaniṣad tries to help us meditate on the one Reality that exists in the form of the worlds of perceivables and conceivables, as the meaning conveyed by one word. Though the world is endlessly extensive, all together it is a systematic whole, a single reality. Similarly, the world of words though endless, could be condensed into one word, and that one word is *auṁ*.

All the words, in all the languages, are composed of letters of their respective alphabets. Such letters consist of both vowels and consonants. In the Sanskrit language, unlike in European languages, the letters of the alphabet are syllables as well. Even though certain vowels can function as words, no consonant on its own, or group of consonants on their own, forms a word; for a consonant needs the enlivening of vowels to make words of them. In other words, the vowels really form the life principle in all written languages. Consonants on their own are merely like inert bodies.

The group of vowels, in the case of the Sanskrit language, begins with "*a*" and ends with "*aḥ*." The one just before "*aḥ*" is "*ṁ*." "*A*" is a sound we have to pronounce with our mouths fully open, and "*ṁ*" with mouths fully closed. The last letter "*aḥ*," a variant version of "*a*," again is to be pronounced with our mouths open. Thus, in respect of articulation, the Sanskrit alphabet begins with a sound uttered with an open mouth, ends with the one uttered with mouth closed, and begins anew with a sound to be uttered with an open mouth. This indicates a cyclic structuring of sounds rather than a linear one, in Sanskrit, resounding the truth that life is a cyclic process rather than a linear one.

The letters that are to be uttered with your mouth open and shut thus come at both extremes of the vowel group of letters of the Sanskrit alphabet. The sound that can be uttered only with your mouth half open and half shut is *u*, which comes almost at the middle of the series of vowels. In a sense, thus, if you condense the vowels of that language into three, they would be *a, u* and *m*. These three letters, if condensed further into one, then become *auṁ*, pronounced *oṁ*, the theme of meditation in the present Upaniṣad.

It is this monosyllable or one word *auṁ* that becomes expanded as the entire world of words, and it is the one *Brahman* or *Ātman* that unfolds itself as all the worlds. Reducing the perceptible world into the world of words, this world of words then into one word of one syllable, and trying to meditatively perceive "everything here" (*idam sarvam*) as an expanded form of this one word, is the epistemological structuring behind the meditation conceived in this Upaniṣad.

The twelve *mantra*s of this Upaniṣad could well be seen as having three sections. The first one consists of the first two *mantra*s and states concisely what Vedānta basically teaches. *"Sarvam hy etad brahma"* (Everything here indeed is *Brahman*), is that essential teaching. This statement is in the form of an equation. How "everything" (*sarvam*) is to be conceived and how it is to be equated with *auṁ* is depicted in the rest of the Upaniṣad.

Auṁ is a word, and "everything" equated to *Brahman* is what this word signifies. A word is called *abhidhāna* (naming), and what it denotes and connotes is *abhidheya* (that which is named). The *abhidheya* side is detailed in *mantras* 3 to 7, and the *abhidhāna* side in *mantras* 8 to 12. Both find a common ground in consciousness, the essential content of *Ātman* or *Brahman*. Meditatively realizing the inseparable oneness of the *abhidhāna-abhidheya* duality, which again is equated with *Brahman*, is what the seeker or, student is meant to achieve. Such is the methodological structuring of this Upaniṣad.

Śaṅkara formulated the Advaita school of Vedānta based mainly on the *Māṇḍūkya Kārikā*, an elucidation of the Vedāntic tenets along with the *Māṇḍūkya Upaniṣad*, its inspirational source. The word *kārikā* means, any versified elucidation of a philosophical or scientific source book. Gauḍapāda, the author of the *Māṇḍūkya Kārikā* was the *guru*'s *guru* of Śaṅkara. The line of *gurus* acknowledged by the tradition of the Advaita system admits Gauḍapāda as the *guru* who comes after Śuka and before Govinda, the direct *guru* of Śaṅkara. But it would be audacious to think that Gauḍapāda was the direct disciple of Śuka, because there has to be a gap between the two for the reason that all the *gurus* mentioned up to Śuka are mythological characters, and from Gauḍapāda onwards they are historical figures. Yet tradition holds that Gauḍapāda was a direct disciple of Śuka.

The line of *gurus* thus honoured is as follows:

nārāyaṇam padmabhavam vasiṣṭham
śaktim ca tat-putra parāśarañca
vyāsam śukam gauḍapadam mahāntam
govinda-yogīndram athāsya śiṣyam
śrī śaṅkarācāryam athāsya padma-
pādañca hastāmalakam ca śiṣyam
tam troṭakam vārtikakāram anyān
asmat gurūn santatam ānatosmi ।

Nārāyaṇa (Viṣṇu), Padmabhava (Brahmā, the Creator), Vasiṣṭha, Śakti, his son Parāśara, Vyāsa, Śuka, Gauḍapāda, Govinda the *yogī*, his disciple Śaṅkara, and followed by Padmapāda, his disciple Hastāmalaka, Troṭaka, and all the other masters, who authored the *vārtikas* — to all these great masters of ours, I pay my homage.

The *Māṇḍūkya Kārikā*, also known as *Gauḍapāda Kārikā*, is meant to be an introductory textbook (*prakaraṇa-grantha*) on Advaita philosophy; and was written as a continuation of the Upaniṣadic thought-line, rather than being an actual commentary on the *Māṇḍūkya Upaniṣad*. The nature of this philosophy as conceivable in modern times has already been made sufficiently clear in our comments on the other nine major Upaniṣads (the one on the *Bṛhadāraṇyaka* was written by Guru Nitya Chaitanya Yati, the present commentator's predecessor in the heirarchy of *gurus* of the Narayana Gurukula Movement), the *Bhagavad Gītā* and the *Vedānta Sūtras* of Narayana Guru, and thus virtually on the *Prasthāna-traya*. Therefore we do not deem it necessary to repeat those comments here. In this commentary we will confine ourselves within the limits of the actual text of the Upaniṣad, without going into the *Māṇḍūkya Kārikā*.

The *Praśna, Muṇḍaka* and *Māṇḍūkya* Upaniṣads, annexed as they are to the *Atharvaveda,* share a common Peace Invocation (*śānti-pāṭha*). A detailed examination of the denotations and connotations of this Peace Invocation was done by us as part of our comments on the *Praśna Upaniṣad,* and therefore it is also not repeated in this commentary.

Śānti-Pāṭha

Peace Invocation

ॐ भद्रं कर्णेभिः शृणुयाम देवा ।
भद्रं पश्येमाक्षभिर्यजत्राः ।
स्थिरैरंगैस्तुष्टुवाँ सस्तनूभिर्
व्यशेम देवहितं यदायुः ॥
स्वस्ति न इन्द्रो वृद्धश्रवाः
स्वस्ति नः पूषा विश्ववेदाः ।
स्वस्ति नस्ताक्ष्र्यो अरिष्टनेमिः
स्वस्ति नो बृहस्पतिर्दधातु ॥
ॐ शान्तिः शान्तिः शान्तिः ॥

oṁ bhadraṁ karṇebhiḥ sṛṇuyāma devā ।
bhadraṁ paśyema akṣabhir yajatrāḥ ।
sthirair aṅgai stuṣṭuvāṁ̐ sastanūbhir
vyaśema devahitam yad āyuḥ ॥
svasti na indro vṛddhaśravāḥ
svasti naḥ pūṣā viśvavedāḥ ।
svasti nas tārkṣyo ariṣṭanemiḥ
svasti no bṛhaspatir dadhātu ॥
oṁ śāntiḥ śāntiḥ śāntiḥ ॥

Auṁ. May we, with our ears hear that which is auspicious, O Gods,
And may we, habitually offering oblations, see with our eyes that which is auspicious.
With strong bodies, singing your praises,

may we live out our span of life destined to us by gods.

May Indra of mature learning bestow well-being on us.

May Pūṣā (the Sun), the knower of all, bestow well-being on us.

May Tārkṣya (Garuḍa), the annihilator of dangers, bestow well-being on us.

May Bṛhaspati bestow well-being on us.

Aum Peace! Peace! Peace!

Māṇḍūkya Upaniṣad

Verse 1

ओमित्येतदक्षरमिदꣳ सर्वं
तस्योपव्याख्यानम्
भूतं भवद्भविष्यदिति
सर्वमोंकार एव ।
यच्चान्यत् त्रिकालातीतं
तदप्योंकार एव ॥

Oṁ ity etad akṣaram idaṁ sarvaṁ
tasyopavyākhyānam
bhūtaṁ bhavad bhaviṣyad iti
sarvam oṁkāra eva ।
yaccānyat trikālātitaṁ
tad apy oṁkāra eva ॥

Auṁ, this syllable is (the imperishable). Its expanded version is all this. All that has happened to be, all that is happening to be, all that will happen to be, all this verily is this syllable *auṁ*. And the other that is beyond the threefold time, too is verily the syllable *auṁ*.

Auṁ (*oṁ*) is the sacred word with which the text of every Upaniṣad customarily begins. And *auṁ,* here, is the word expanded as the essential teaching of Vedānta. In both these respects the word/syllable *auṁ* is quite significant.

Auṁ is first stated as *akṣara,* a word meaning a letter of the alphabet or a syllable that forms a part or the whole of a word. As an *abhidhāna* (a word that signifies something) *auṁ* is a word formed of one syllable. And as *abhidheya* (that which is signified) the same *auṁ* is the imperishable Reality. In this latter sense, the word *akṣara* is the opposite of *kṣara,* meaning "that which is perishable." *Akṣara* thus means the imperishable Reality. The word *akṣara* is thus used here in two senses, one relevant in the world of words, and the other in what the words signify.

The world, an aggregate of "everything" (*sarvam*), is then perceived as the expanded version of the one imperishable Reality (*akṣaram*) on the *abhidheya* side, and as signified by the monosyllable (*akṣaram*) *auṁ* on the *abhidhāna* side.

How the syllable/word *auṁ* represents the imperishable Reality and everything perishable simultaneously is what the Upaniṣad tries to expound. In an expanded sense, the *abhidheya* side includes everything perishable as well, because all such are nothing but the manifest forms of the imperishable.

Let us now see how the imperishable and everything perishable are related:

It is the visible world and its impermanence that make us think of what is real. We also form part of that perishable world, but each of us feels, the "I" in us continues to exist unchanged in spite of all the constant changes that our external appearance undergoes. The same should be true with the world as a whole. In spite of the incessant change everything in the world is subject to, something that is aware of these changes, as in "my" own case, should exist. This something has to be a conscious reality or consciousness itself, and functionally it finds expression individually as well as universally, while it, remaining unchanging, knows all changes. This Reality, according to Vedānta, is the consciousness aspect of the imperishable. It is not just a conscious reality, but is Consciousness itself and is denoted by the word *cit*.

The changefulness of my appearance not withstanding. I am aware that I endure in and through these changes. What we call birth and death being part of these changes, what endures should transcend both birth and death. So too with the universal existence. The one Reality that knows all that happens in the world should existentially surpass all the changes, surpassing even the creation and dissolution of the world. This ever existing Reality is signified by the term *sat*, meaning "Existence," in Vedānta.

I thus know myself as existing, and I know myself as knowing. Over and above this, I feel pleasure and pain, and I have likes and dislikes; in short, I evaluate everything I happen to know in relation to my own existence and my sense of meaning. This aspect of my being is called *ānanda* (Happiness or Value sense). Universally too, the same *ānanda* aspect should be there in the all-inclusive and all-knowing Existence. The appearance of the world itself is thought of as an external expression of the self-amusement (*līlā*) or sporting of the one Reality.

All these pertain to the Imperishable (*akṣara*) as well as to its expanded version, and for this reason the Imperishable often is defined as *sat-cit-ānanda* (Existence-Consciousness-Value sense). This *sat-cit-ānanda* is what unfolds itself as my individuated existence, my knowing and my value experiences, as well as the universal existence of the cosmic system, the universal knowing function and the universal value experiences such as happiness and sufferings that generally form part of life. What this *sat-cit-ānanda* unfolds itself as, both in such individuated and universal aspects at the same time, is the *upavyākhyāna* (expanded version) understood here.

All phenomenal appearances result from the self-unfoldment of the *akṣara*, and in the *Bhagavad Gītā* are referred to as *bhāva*s, meaning "becoming" or 'that which has emerged'. Then the *akṣara*-Reality is itself called *sat* (the word *sat*, it is to be noted, is used here to mean *sat-cit-ānanda* inclusively). Then how are *sat* and *bhāva* related? The *Gītā* makes this point clear in its verse II.16 as follows:

nāsato vidyate bhāvo
nābhāvo vidyate sataḥ ।
ubhayor api dṛṣtontas
tvanayos tattvadarśibhiḥ. ॥

The unreal (*asat*) does not manifest itself. The Real (*sat*) never remains without manifesting itself. The inherent Truth in these two has thus been perceived by the seers of ultimate Reality.

The *akṣara*, thus, does not remain without itself expanding as everything in all the worlds, and conversely, everything in all the worlds cannot appear to be without the *akṣara* Reality remaining unseen, yet underlying them. To put the same in the usual Vedāntic terms, the inperceptible *Brahman* or *Ātman* never remains an abstract Reality without itself manifesting as the perceptible world; and the perceptible world connot appear to be without *Brahman* or *Ātman* imperceptibly underlying all of them. *Brahman,* thus, is to be actually perceived in the form of the world. It is comparable to the relationship between gold and ornament forms. Gold as the indestructible substance never remains without having a destructible assumed form like that of an ornament. Likewise, no ornament form can appear without the existence of the gold substance. The imperishable gold and the perishable ornament form never remain separate. Their separateness exists only in our minds as ideas. So too, *Brahman* exists by assummig the form of the world and the world's appearance has *Brahman* for its substance. The inseparable oneness of *Brahman* and the world is really the essential content of *advaita* (non-duality) proper. The separateness of the two is a creation of the conditioned state of our mind, called *avidyā* or nescience. Intuitively perceiving this oneness marks the final attainment of a seer of the ultimate Reality or a *yogī.*

"All this" (*idam sarvam*) which is an expanded form of the *akṣaram,* is comprised of not merely the physical world; it on the other hand, is inclusive of the physical entities and the mental concepts, both matter and mind, both object and subject, both the external and the internal and both cause and effect.

Bhūtam, Bhavat, Bhaviṣyat

The "all" or "everything" (*sarvam*) is in a state of constant change. Every change involves events. Without events taking place or in a state of standstill, we would have no sense of time. Even the internal sense of our enduring is a feeling of the continuity of our internal states of change. All such changes take place in what really exists, in the *sat* aspect of *saccidānanda*, and itself remains aware of all such changes because of the function of the *cit* aspect of it. This knowing function relates one event with those that follow, and the continuity of it creates the sense of time. In short, time is a sense created by the *cit*'s function of knowing the events that take place in *sat*.

This time-sense customarily is divided by us into three — past, present and future. *Bhūtam, bhavat* and *bhaviṣyat* are the terms the Upaniṣad uses to signify this threefold division of time. All derived from the verb root *bhū*, meaning "to exist" or "to become"; *bhūtam*, means "that which has happened," *bhavat* means "that which is happening" and *bhaviṣyat* means "that which is yet to happen." This clearly shows how the happening of events and our time-sense are closely related.

This threefold division of time becomes meaningful only in a relative sense. Absolutely speaking, the incessant flow of events or of time-sense alone is real.

Let us look at these divisions closely. What is meant by the present? It is simply a thin film that separates the past from the future. This thin film has no thickness. If time is conceived as a line, then the present is like a point that has no measurement. Looked at thus, that is logically, only the past and the future have being; the present has no being of its own.

What is then the nature of the past that we experience? It is in the form of memories of the events that we have passed through. Where do such memories have their being? Only as our present experience, as we can memorize the past only in the present. Experientially we can never live in the past.

What now is the nature of the future? It is merely in the form of our expectations of events yet to take place. Such expectations have their being in consciousness only at the present, never in the future. We can only imagine our life tomorrow, but when lived that tomorrow becomes today.

The past thus exists in the present; the future also exists in the present. The present alone thus is the experienced time. This present is simply a moving forward of the thin film that separates the future from the past. It is therefore called the eternal present. Experientially, the time that exists thus is present alone, and logically the other two alone.

The threefold division of time, thus, is relative in this sense, as well as in the sense that the time sense always depends upon events. Events, in their turn, take place in the being of *sarvam* (everything), which is nothing more than the expanded version (*upa-vyākhyānam*) of the *akṣaram* or *auṁ*. And to that extent, the threefold time is also not outside the ambit of *auṁ*.

Trikālātītam

The threefold time, we have already seen, results from serially arranging in our knowledge the events that take place in life. Its real place is in consciousness. This consciousness that experiences the threefold time transcends this division. Consciousness (*cit*) in turn is the essential content of *Ātman* or *Brahman*. Consciousness, *Ātman* or *Brahman*, thus is *trikālātītam* (that which transcends the threefold time).

This first *mantra* thus equates *auṁ*, the *akṣaram* or the imperishable, to all (*sarvaṁ*) that is perishable. That means, it is the one eternal Reality that appears as all the transient forms that emerge and remerge, which are what constitute the apparent world. Thus the two are inseparably one. The imperishable Reality remains imperishable while the perishable configurations of Itself appear and disappear in It, and this phenomenon is what we experience as the world.

The next *mantra* equates this "everything" (*sarvam*) with *Brahman* and then with *Ātman.*

Verse 2

सर्वं॰ ह्येतद् ब्रह्म
अयमात्मा ब्रह्म
सोऽयमात्मा चतुष्पात् ॥

sarvaṁ hy etad brahma
ayam ātmā brahma
so 'yam ātmā catuṣpāt ॥

All this, verily, is *Brahman.*
This Self is *Brahman.*
This Self, being such, has four quarters.

Sarvam (everything), that was seen as the expanded version of the *akṣaraṁ auṁ*, first is equated here to *Brahman*. This *Brahman,* then, is equated to *Ātman,* and finally this *Ātman* being Consciousness (*cit*) in essence, is stated as having four quarters or legs.

The "*sarvam*" understood here, as we have already noticed, does not exclude anything from its ambit. Both mind and matter, body and soul, cause and effect, the gross and the subtle, the immanent and the transcendental, *parā* and *aparā* — all are included in it. All the countless worlds conceived by modern astrophysics, and all the fourteen or twenty-one worlds supposed by the Indian mythology, are not outside it. The tripartite factors of knowledge, called *tripuṭi*, — the knower, the known and knowledge — are also so. In short, nothing perceivable or conceivable is excluded from it.

This *sarvam* is first equated to *Brahman*. That means, *Brahman* is the Reality that appears as *sarvam*. The *Taittirīya Upaniṣad* defines "*Brahman* as that from which these beings are born; that by which, when born, they live; that into which, when going back, they enter" (III.1). That means, *Brahman* is the Substance from which everything originates with no other efficient cause, as a form of which everything lives, and into which everything merges back upon dissolution.

That this Substance is *sat-cit-ānanda* we have already noticed. Of these three defining factors of *Brahman*, the *cit* (consciousness) aspect is what is taken into account here. How the ultimate Reality is unconditioned Consciousness in essence is clarified by Narayana Guru by resorting to the modern analytical method as follows:

> Cloths are nothing but yarns;
> Yarns are nothing but fibres;
> Fibres are nothing but primeval
> Elements clinging together;
> This way of search,
> Extended to its extreme,
> Reveals that everything becomes apparent
> Out of one Consciousness;
> As is flowing water (mirage)
> Seen in a desert land.
> Ultimately what exists thus
> Is Consciousness alone. — *Advaita Dīpikā* v. 3

The word "*brahman*" is derived from the verb root *bṛh*

meaning "to grow" (*bṛhi vṛddhan*). *Brahman* thus literally is the Reality that is always in the process of growing (*bṛṁhati iti brahma*). That means, the emanation of everything happens in the Substance, *Brahman*. Appearance of some facet of existence means the disappearance of some other facet. *Brahman* thus is the Substance in which the never ending process of emergence and remergence of individuated apparent forms happen.

Brahman as such is formless, as gold is when considered as substance. All the latter's visible forms are those of ornaments. Gold as a substance has no form of its own and thus is formless, and for this reason invisible. *Brahman*, likewise, though the one undeniable Reality behind all that appears to form the world, is formless and thus invisible.

Brahman being the one Substance in the being of everything in all the worlds, the Substance in the being of myself, the knower or seeker, also is the very same *Brahman* Consciousness in essence. Knowing *Brahman* as an object is not possible, because it is not an object knowable to the subject, but is the Substance that underlies the being of both the subject and the object. But there is a direct way of having *Brahman*-awareness — the knower inwordly experiencing *Brahman* as the Consciousness-Substance in his or her own being.

"I" is the word with which every individual knower refers to himself or herself. The philosophical term for the word "I" in Vedānta is *ātman* or *ātmā*. Therefore oneself is referred to as *ātman*. Experientially knowing *ātman* or oneself means, being aware, "I am *Brahman* is essential content." It is just like a piece of ornament that realizes, "I am gold." Being experientially realizable as oneself or as *ātman*,

Brahman is itself referred to as *Ātman* in the Upaniṣads. This is justifiable etymologically also, because the word "*ātman*" means "that which pervades the being of something." The word is derived from the verb-root *āt* meaning "to pervade" (*ād vyāpane*). In the gold and ornament analogy, gold is the substance that pervades the being of the ornament, and therefore gold is the *ātmā* and the ornament form is the body (*śarīra*). Such is the way, according to Advaita Vedānta, *ātmā* and *śarīra* are related. Likewise, *Brahman* exists as the Substance in every individual being to form its *ātmā*, and this individuated form is called *śarīra* which literally means "that which perishes." As the Substance that pervades the being of the entire cosmic system or all the worlds, the same *ātmā* is referred to as *paramātmā* or the Supreme or Transcendental Self (*Ātmā*). Every individual realizing oneself (*ātman*) as *Brahman* is cited in this *mantra* as "*ayam ātmā brahma*" (This self is *Brahman*).

The Great Dicta

"*Ayam ātmā brahma*" actually is one of the great dicta (*mahā-vākyas*) of Vedānta. These dicta declare in a condensed form what Vedānta essentially teaches. The present one, coming as it is as part of the *Māṇḍūkya Upaniṣad*, appended to the *Atharvaveda*, is traditionally considered to contain the wisdom teaching of the whole of this Veda. Similarly, the other three come under the other three Vedas, and therefore are counted as the condensed form of the wisdom teaching of each respective Veda.

The great dictum "*tat tvam asi*" (That thou art) appears in the *Chāndogya Upaniṣad* that forms part of the literature following the *Sāmaveda* tradition. "*Aham brahma asmi*" (I am *Brahman*) is the dictum that belongs to the Yajurvedic tradition and appears in the *Bṛhadāraṇyaka Upaniṣad*. The *Aitareya Upaniṣad*, annexed to the *Ṛgveda*, has in it the dictum *"prajñānan brahma"* (*Brahman* is Consciousness).

All these four dicta take the form of equations. One limb of each equation represents the individuated aspect of being and the other the universal. The only exception is the dictum *"prajñānam brahma"* (*Brahman* is Consciousness) where the stress is on the essential context of *Brahman*. These dicta, in short, clarify that, what is essentially real in an individuated being (I, you or this self) is the essential content in the universal being also. That the essential content is pure and unconditioned Consciousness (*prajñānam*) is stated in the fourth dictum *"prajñānam brahma."*

How to understand the oneness of the individual being and the universal being has been a matter of detailed study in the traditional Śaṅkara school of Vedānta. This particular section is known as *mahā-vākya-nirūpaṇa* (discussion on the meaning of the great dicta). The great dictum *tat tvam asi* is traditionally taken to represent all four dicta in the context of any detailed study of these.

Though the available introductory textbooks of Vedānta (*prakaraṇa-granthas*), now attributed to Śaṅkara, give much importance to a detailed semantic analysis of the dictum *tat tvam asi*, Śaṅkara does not himself make such an argument or analysis in his commentary on the *mantras* of the *Chāndogya Upaniṣad* in which the dictum actually appears. Had Śaṅkara been serious about such a study, he should have done it when commenting on the *Chāndogya Upaniṣad*. It, therefore, is to be presumed that the *prakaraṇa-granthas* of Vedānta, now considered as authored by Śaṅkara, must have been composed by some of his scholarly successors. They were also known as Śaṅkarācāryas because they were the heads of the monasteries founded by the original Śaṅkara. Admitting that Consciousnes is the essential content of what exists individually as well as universally, makes all such pedantic exercises that examine the *vācyārtha* (literal meaning) and *lakṣaṇārtha* (indirect or suggested meaning) of the terms *tat* (That) and *tvam* (you), unwarranted.

Another peculiarity noticeable with these dicta is that one limb of the three are pronouns, of first person ("*aham*" of *aham brahma asmi*), second person ("*tvam*" of *tat tvam asi*); and third person ("*ayam*" of *ayam ātmā brahma*). It shows that whether you treat the individual being referable as first person, second person or third person, it is, in essential content, *prajñānam* (Consciousness) that occupies the place of a pronoun in the other dictum.

The following five *mantra*s analyse the functional states of Consciousness or *prajñanam.* It shows how important perceiving the all-underlying Reality as Consciousness (*prajñānam* or *cit*) is. One's own experience of self-existence is also an enduring consciousness. It is this enduring consciousness that is stated to have four quarters or legs.

"*Pāda*" is the word used here to denote quarters or feet. What these feet are will be clarified in the coming *mantra*s. Derived from the root *pad,* meaning "to lead forward" (*pada gatau*), the word "*pāda*" signifies "that which makes you reach the goal," or "the attainment of the goal." The goal here is to attain a comprehensive vision of *sarvam* (everything) as *Brahman*, and the means resorted to here is the analysis of the functional states of Consciousness, the essential content of *Brahman.*

We saw at the beginning of the Upaniṣad, a series of equations, i.e., *auṁ* or *akṣaram* = *sarvam* = *Brahman* = *Ātman,* were presented. *Ātmā,* as we know, is pure Consciousness in essence. Hence a structural analysis of the functional states of Consciousness enables us to visualize how these series of equations comprehensively includes everything (*sarvam*).

Now begins the analysis:

Verse 3

जागरितस्थानो बहिःप्रज्ञः
सप्ताङ्ग एकोनविंशतिमुखः
स्थूलभुग्वैश्वानरः प्रथमः पादः ॥

jāgarita sthāno bahiḥ prajñaḥ
saptāṅga eko-na-viṁśati-mukhaḥ
sthūlabhug vaiśvānaraḥ prathamaḥ pādaḥ ॥

The first quarter or foot is Vaiśvānara, whose sphere of activity is the waking state, whose knowledge is outwardly oriented, who has seven limbs, who has nineteen facets, and who enjoys gross objects.

Jāgarita (waking), *svapna* (dreaming), *suṣupti* (deep sleep) and *turīya* (the fourth or the transcendental) are the states of consciousness examined in *mantra*s 3 to 7 in order that we may get a comprehensive vision of "*sarvam,*" the self-unfolded apparent form of *Brahman*. These four states, we know, are the functional modes of Consciousness, the essential content of *Brahman* or *Ātman*. How are *Ātman* and Consciousness related? Is it as substance and attribute? No; the essential content of *Ātman* is itself Consciousness. That means, *Ātman* is to be understood or rather realized as one's enduring self-consciousness. How the one is to be understood in terms of the other is made clear by Narayana Guru as follows:

> Pure Consciousness and "I" (*Ātmā*) —
> These two are one alone
> In the perception of the one
> Who has become free of the veil of (*māyā*);
> Others go on arguing for or against.
> If "I" (*Ātmā*) could be taken as something
> Other than pure Consciousness,
> Then there would be no one to be conscious
> Of that Consciousness.
>
> — *Ātmopadeśa Śatakam*, v. 99

The functions of consciousness, in fact, are not compartmentalizable as these four. Infinite really are the potentials hidden in consciousness. The four states mentioned here are simply four clearly discernible stages in the never ending oscillation of consciousness between two extemities — the *Jāgarita* (waking) and *turīya* (the fourth) states. Derived from the verb root *jagṛ*, meaning "to be having no sleep" (*jagari nidrā-kṣaye*), *Jāgarita* is the state in which no sleep is felt. Is there in our actual life a state of consciousness when no taint of sleep at all is present? No, even in our fully alert state there would be at least a trace of sleep. If this state of alertness continues beyond a certain limit, the alert state will slowly give way to sleepiness. This sleepiness should be present in what we call the fully alert state also, though to a lesser degree. No one can claim to exist in a state of wakefulness without a touch of sleepiness. That means, a fully waking state is something never attainable by anyone in actual life, except perhaps, by some perfect *yogīs*.

Turīya too, as we shall see in *mantra* 7, is a state only experienced by great *yogīs*, but not by ordinary people. The word *turīya* just means "the fourth" or having four parts. *Caturtha* (the fourth) is the word used in the Upaniṣad instead.

The function of consciousnsness thus is a process of oscillation, like that of a clock's pendulum, between full *Jāgarita* and full *turīya*, both extremities never touched. It is then for convenience sake that four noticeable stages are marked in this study. Narayana Guru, in his *Ātmopadeśa Śatakam* verse 36, also states clearly that the potentials hidden in consciousness are limitless.

Of four such discernible states, *Jāgarita* is the sphere of activity of Vaiśvānara. A compound word, *vaiśvānara* has in it two words, *vaiśva* and *nara*. *Vaiśva* means "that which is related to *viśva* (the cosmic system or the whole)." Vaiśvānara, thus, means, "the whole having become an individual human being," the word *nara* meaning "an individual human." *Vaiśva*, thus, pertains to the universal (*samaṣṭi*) and *nara* to the particular (*vyaṣṭi*). If these two form the two extreme poles of a situation, then Vaiśvānara is the unitive or non-dual Consciousness functioning in the waking state. This life-situation forms the *Jāgarita* sphere of activity of consciousness.

The waking state could thus be seen as having two dimensions: the particular and the universal. The particular dimension is what we are familiar with as our own waking state. In this state, we remain conscious of what happens outside of us (*bahiḥ prajñaḥ*). Likewise, a waking state of the universal consciousness, that could be called *viśvātmā*, is also to be visualized, in order to keep our perception well balanced and comprehensive. This state of consciousness could be seen as remaining aware of what goes on all through the world with an outwardly oriented perception (*bahiḥ-prajñaḥ*).

The peculiarity of the waking state, whether considered in the universal context or the particular, is that it is outwardly oriented (*bahiḥ prajñaḥ*). That means, it remains conscious of everything outside, yet is unaware of itself. A subject can know objects while being ignorant of what the subject is. Such is the nature of the waking state. All such objects put together form the world or *viśva;* and the individual subject who knows this *viśva* is a human being or *nara*. The *viśva* becoming known to *nara* is what happens at the waking state (*Jāgarita*), and such is the way Vaiśvānara becomes the first *pāda* of consciousness functioning in the *Jāgarita* state.

This Vaiśvānara is *sthūlabhuk,* the one who enjoys gross objects, *sthūla* means "gross," and *bhuk* or *bhoktā* "the enjoyer." The self in its waking state, called here Vaiśvānara, has three different functions of knowing, doing actions and enjoying. These functions respectively are known as *jñātṛtva* (being the knower), *kartṛtva* (being the doer of actions) and *bhoktṛtva* (being the enjoyer). All these three are to be treated as inclusively covered by the word *bhuk,* meaning *bhoktā* or the enjoyer and all are related to the gross (*sthūla*) aspect of existence.

The self, being such, as the *jñātā* or knower, in the waking state, becomes conscious of external gross objects, sound (*śabda*), touch (*sparśa*), form (*rūpa*), taste (*rasa*) and smell (*gandha*). These objects together are called *viṣayas,* and objects are the distinguishing qualities respectively of the five gross elements (*sthūla-bhūtas*), space (*ākāśa*), air (*vāyu*), fire (*agni* or *tejas*), water (*ap*) and earth (*pṛthivī*). The above said five objects are grasped by the five sense organs (*jñānendriyas*), ears (*śravaṇa*), skin (*tvak*), eyes (*cakṣus* or *netra*), tongue (*rasana*) and nose (*ghrāṇa*).

Each of these sense organs, Vedānta holds, is the individuated subtle form of the concerned universal gross element. For example, the sense organ ear is the individuated subtle form of the gross element space; the sense organ skin is the individuated subtle form of the gross element air, and so on. All these together are nothing more than the variant manifest forms of the one *Ātmā*. This explains why sense organs and the respective objects can come into contact with one another, resulting in the concerned sense perception. Such perceptions, according to Vedānta, are really events in which the non-dual oneness of Consciousness is unconsciously realized upon the sense organ forgoing the particular conditioning factors that make them sense organs and the objects forgoing the particular conditioning factors that make them objects. The forgoing of such conditioning factors results in the revelation that one Consciousness or *Ātmā* is the common ground of the sense organs and the sense objects. This realization of oneness is what we, because of our ignorance, count as sense perceptions.

Likewise, the *kartā* (doer) aspect of the self depends for its function on the organs of action known as *karmendriyas*. These are speech (*vāk*), hands (*pāṇi*), feet (*pāda*), excretory organ (*pāyu*) and genitals (*upastha*). These organs of action also have their respective objects, namely, words for speech, things grasped for hands, walking for feet, faeces for excretory organs and sex for genitals. The actions performed by these organs take place in our gross body (*sthūla-śarīra*), a manifestation of the gross imagination (*sthūla-saṁkalpanā*) of the Self. How and where *karma*s (actions) take place is portrayed by the *Bhagavad Gītā* as follows:

> *prakṛteḥ kriyamānāni*
> *guṇaiḥ karmāṇi sarvaśah* ।
> *ahaṁkāra-vimūḍhātmā*
> *kartāham iti manyate* ॥ — III. 27

> Actions in every way take place because of the *guṇa*s of *prakṛti*. Deluded by the I sense, one holds, "I am the doer."

Narayana Guru also, in the very first verse of the *Karma-darśana* (Vision by Actions) of his *Darśana-mālā* (Garland of Visions) says:

> *ātmaiva māyayā karma*
> *karoti bahurūpa-dhṛk* ।
> *asaṁgaḥ svaprakāśo 'pi*
> *nidrāyām iva taijasaḥ* ॥

> *Ātmā* alone, while being completely unattached to anything and self-luminous, performs all the *karma*s by assuming various forms, by virtue of its own *māyā*, as does *taijasa* in the sleeping state.

All *karma*s that take place in the individual being or in the universal being thus really happen in the Self (*Ātmā*) because of its own *māyā*. *Karma*s, in other words, are the *kṛti* (creative potential) of *Ātmā* become actualized. *Ātmā* in that state is known as *prakṛti*. And in the waking state, all the *karma*s are perceived to take place in the gross (*sthūla*) aspect of *prakṛti* or Nature.

The event of enjoying also, likewise, involves an enjoyer (*bhoktā*) and an object enjoyed (*bhogya-viṣaya*). These two are also merely the same *prakṛti* (Nature) become apparent subjectively and objectively. Narayana Guru says:

> "Nature (*prakṛti*), undergoing division within itself,
> Appears on the one side as the enjoyer,
> And on the other, as the world of enjoyables,
> That arouses this-sense, manifesting extensively,
> Both as here and hereafter.
>
> — *Ātmopadeśa Śatakam,* verse 81

Whether as *jñāna* (knowledge), *karma* (actions) or *bhoga* (enjoyment), all the functions of consciousness in its waking state imply the tripartite factors known as *tripuṭi,* i.e. the knower, the known and knowledge, the doer, the doing and the done, the enjoyer, enjoyment and the enjoyed. The one *Ātmā* that manifests itself as all these is beyond this tripartite division.

Being externally oriented (*bahiḥ-prajñaḥ*), the knower (*jñātā*) in the waking state remains ignorant of who and what he is inside; the doer (*kartā*) remains ignorant of who and what he is inside; and the enjoyer (*bhoktā*) remains ignorant of who and what he is inside. Had the *jñātā, kartā* and *bhoktā* the opportunity to know himself inwardly, he would have attained the experiential awareness of the ultimate Reality he really is, while knowing, doing and enjoying.

The *jñātṛtva* (the state of being a knower), *kartṛtva* (the state of being a doer of actions) and *bhoktṛtva* (the state of being an enjoyer) are functions of consciousness in the waking state, and do not take place unless inwardly supported by the functions of the mental faculties known as *antaḥkaraṇas*. *Manas* (mind), *buddhi* (intellect or reasoning capacity), *citta* (memorizing and recalling) and *ahaṁkāra* (I-sense) are these faculties according to Indian psychologists. The function of *manas* is to doubt, imagine and ask question. *Buddhi* reasons with the help of memories stored and recalled by *citta,* and *ahaṁkāra* evaluates what is thus known in terms of values, i.e. as pleasant, unpleasant and indifferent.

There is another set of internal bodily functions that makes all the wakeful functions of consciousness possible. These are the *prāṇa*s or vital airs. *Prāṇa* functions at the same time in five different domains, and hence the name *pañca-prāṇa*s, the fivefold *prāṇa*s: *prāṇa, apāna, vyāna, udāna* and *samāna.*

The functions of these five *prāṇa*s are conceived differently in various Upaniṣads and introductory textbooks. The *Vivekacūḍāmaṇi* attributed to Śaṅkara says, inhalation and exhalation, yawning, sneezing, excretion and leaving this body are the activities of the five *prāṇa*s (see verse 102). We quote below the portion of the *Praśna Upaniṣad* where these *prāṇa*s are conceived as functioning in yet another way, related rather to subtler contexts of wisdom.

> As an emperor commands his officials saying, "Govern such and such districts," even so this *prāṇa* directs other *prāṇa*s in their respective functions.
>
> To the excretory organ and genitals (is directed) *apāna* (the downward vital function). *Prāṇa* himself functions in the eyes and ears, in the mouth and nose. *Samāna*

> (equalizing vital function) that distributes indeed equitably whatever is offered as food, is directed to the middle region; from it arise the seven flames.
>
> In the heart is this (*samāna*'s) self. From here are issued one hundred and one arteries. Of each one of them are issued a hundred smaller arteries. Of each of these branches are issued seventytwo thousand sub-branches. Within all these move *vyāna* (the diffused breath).
>
> Now, *udāna* (the upward breath) is that which moves upwards alone. Following meritorious deeds it leads to the world of merits; following sinful deeds it leads to the world of sins. Following both kinds of deeds it leads to the human world.
>
> The sun, verily, as the externally manifest *prāṇa,* rises gracing the *prāṇa* of eyes. The divinity in the earth seizes *apāna* in man. What is in between (the sun and the earth) is *samāna* and air is *vyāna.*
>
> Fire verily is *udāna*. Because of it, one, whose lusture has died out with senses sunk in mind, re-emerges.
>
> As one's thinking is, so he attains *prāṇa. Prāṇa* functions undiffentiated from lustre. Along with *Ātmā* it leads the world as mind conceives it. — III.4-10

Since a detailed study of these functions has been made by us in our commentary on the *Praśna Upaniṣad,* we do not repeat it here.

The five sense organs (*jñānendriyas*), the five organs of action (*karmendriyas*), the five *prāṇas* along with the four mental faculties (*antaḥkaraṇas*) function together in the waking state.

Such is the sphere of activities of Vaiśvānara, and it is stated here to have seven limbs (*saptāṅgaḥ*). Which these limbs are, is a matter of speculation. The only available guiding suggestion in other scriptures in this respect is a citation in the *Chāndogya Upaniṣad* describing a picture of Vaiśvānara. It says:

> Of this *vaiśvānara-ātmā, sutejas* (the world of brightness or heaven) is the crown of the head; *viśvarūpa* (the sun) is the eye; *pṛthagvartmā* (air) is the *prāṇa; bahula* (space) is the trunk; *rayi* (water) is the urinary bladder; the earth is the feet. Its chest forms the sacrificial altar; hairs form the *kuśa*-grass; heart forms the *gārhapatyāgni;* mind forms the *dakṣiṇāgni;* mouth forms the *āhavanīyagni.* — V.18.2

If the sacrificial altar and the three sacrificial fires could be considered as forming one unit, then the number of limbs become seven. These limbs, as noticed earlier, show a series of correlations between the universal and particular aspects of existence. The world of brightness or heaven pertains to the universal, and crown of the head to the individual; the sun is of the universal existence and eye of the particular; air is universal and *prāṇa* particular; space is universal and trunk of the body particular; water is universal and urinary bladder particular; the earth is universal and feet particular; sacrificial fire belongs to the universal and chest region to the individual. The real Vaiśvānara, therefore, is to be intuitively perceived as having a universal dimension at one pole and an individual dimension at the other.

Vaiśvānara, the state of consciousness functioning in the waking state, is considered here to have nineteen faces. Difficult indeed is counting the number of ways in which consciousness functions in this state. Whichever way it functions, the consciousness within has to have outlets to come out and be in contact with the external objects that pertain to the universal aspect of existence. Such outlets are known as *karaṇa*s, meaning instruments, and are counted here as nineteen, and therefore these are considered the nineteen faces or moths (*mukha*) of Vaiśvānara. These are the five sense-organs — ears, skin, eyes, tongue and nose, five organs of action — speech, hands, feet, excretory organs and genitals, five *prāṇa*s — *prāṇa, apāna, vyāna, udāna* and *samāna,* and the four *antaḥkaraṇa*s or mental faculties *manas, buddhi, citta* and *ahaṁkāra.* The nature of the function of each of these has already been examined. Put otherwise, each individual gets into contact with the universal aspects of existence in the waking state through these nineteen outlets, resulting in the consciousness becoming functionally manifest.

Verse 4

स्वप्नस्थानोऽन्तःप्रज्ञः
सप्ताङ्ग एकोनविंशतिमुखः
प्रविविक्तभुक् तैजसो द्वितीयः पादः ॥

svapna-sthāno 'ntaḥprajñaḥ
saptāṅga ekonaviṁśati-mukhaḥ
praviviktabhuk taijaso dvitīyaḥ pādaḥ ॥

The second quarter is Taijasa, whose sphere of activity is the dream state, whose knowledge is inwardly oriented, who has seven limbs, who has nineteen facets, and who enjoys very solitary objects.

The second quarter of the domain of functional consciousness is Taijasa whose sphere of activities is the *svapna* state. *Svap* is the root from which the word *svapna* is derived, and it means, "to sleep," "to repose" (*ñjiṣvap-śaye*). Though the word *svapna* literally means "sleep," as denoting a state of consciousness as understood in Indian psychology, it signifies the dream state. The word used to indicate dreamless deep sleep is *suṣupti*, again derived from the same root, and is the third quarter described in the next two *mantras*.

Dreaming has been much studied by different schools of psychology, but with no definite conclusion arrived at. Dictionaries of dreams have even been published by psychologists as an attempt at dream interpretation. In spite of all these efforts, dreaming remains a mystery, just as the world does. It is also not definite whether this phenomenon is natural with human beings alone, or is common to all living beings. It is indefinite because of the fact that dreaming is an experience not shareable with or perceptible to anyone else. This is indicated by the epithet *praviviktabhuk* (the one who enjoys very solitary objects) of the *mantra*. Even when we try our best to give expression to what we feel within, no expression enables someone else to perceive fully what we feel within, whatever be the means of expression like language, art and the rest. Such is the nature of the subjective world known inwardly (*antaḥ-prajñaḥ*).

What is connoted by the term *svapna* or dream seen inwardly therefore is not to be understood as signifying merely the experience we ordinarily call dreaming. It, on the other hand, includes all that is known inwardly (*antaḥ-prajñaḥ*). This inwardly known world is inconceivably extensive. Besides what we term dreaming, the world of ideas and ideals, reasoning, imagination, creative imagination, value notions, day-dreaming and innumerable other mental functions that are outwardly invisible, are to be understood comprehensively by the term *svapna,* the sphere of activities of Taijasa.

We encounter external objects in our waking state. Every such encounter results in the forming of a corresponding idea, known as *pratibhā,* in our mind. How such experiences affect our own life is evaluated with a value sense each possesses. This value sense is yet another subjective phenomenon. Sense perception, value notions, past memories and many such factors are put together into a sort of melting pot by the faculty of reasoning, yet another of the subjective phenomena. This reasoning faculty, through inference and other such means of knowledge, known in Indian epistemology as *pramāṇa*s, creates new knowledges and ideas, sometimes even creative images. All these are not outside the extensiveness of *svapna* to be understood in this *mantra.* The worlds created by such subjective creative imaginations are really limitless.

Our institutions of higher education try to outstretch the outer boundaries of this world of dreams. All libraries are the external store-houses of such internal dreams given expression to through the medium of language. All forms of art are the expressions of such dreams. The reach of this world is always on the increase; so too is the expanding universe known to modern physics and perceived in the waking state.

Now what about our actual dreams? Though psychologists fail to define this subjective phenomenon, our experience is that each one's dreams reflect one's past experiences, future expectations, hopes and aspirations in life, fears, value notions, unresolved problems, the mystery of life, the inability of our mind to face certain problems in life — in short all that pertains to the subjective world. The only definition we can give to dreaming therefore is this: it is a state of consciousness in which mind creates the objects to be enjoyed within itself by the same mind.

As was stated earlier in our comments on *mantra* 3, no one experiences in actual life either the fully awakened state or the state of fully deep sleep. The latter is a state in which one is conscious of nothing, and therefore nothing can be said about it. Being so, no one can claim, "I have experienced the real deep sleep and it is such and such." Consciousness in our actual life thus oscillates between the fully awakened and fully deep sleep states, never touching either end at any time. Thus, having never experienced the fully awaking state and the fully deep sleeping state, all our life-experiences, including the supposed realitie experienced in the waking state, are a sort of prolonged dream.

We usually hold that everything we encounter in our waking state is real and all that is seen in dreams is unreal. Really, both are states of the same consciousness, one state being absent when the other is functioning. Treating one as real and the other as unreal, therefore, makes no sense. The only difference is that the objects seen in the waking state exist externally, whereas in dreams they exist internally. Both are experiences the same mind has. On closer examination we see that everything that we consider as external objects exists only as modes of expression of consciousness or mind. We do not intend to go into the details of this aspect, as we have made it sufficiently clear in our other works.* Summarizing this point, Narayana Guru says:

> From the one pure and unconditioned Consciousness
> Arise countless sparks creating the impression
> Of the existent and the non-existent alike,
> Which together constitute the world.
> And thus, it is to be realized,
> Nothing has being apart from the beingness.
> Of one pure Consciousness or *Ātmā.*
> This enlightenment would reveal
> The unitiveness of Truth.
>
> — *Atmopadeśa Śatakam,* v. 89

Again the *Asatya-darśana* (Vision through Non-existence) of his *Darśana-Mālā* (Garland of Visions) begins with the line *"manomayam idam sarvam"* (Everything here indeed is imaginative mind in essence).

In short, what we think of as the existing external world also has a dream-like existence. A story in the *Yoga-Vāsiṣṭha* shows how meaningless it is to consider the experiences of the waking state as real and those of dreaming as unreal:

There was brāhmin who had only one child, and for the same reason, the child was much loved by him. One day the father had an afternoon nap and saw a dream while asleep. In the dream he became a king, had a luxurious life with nine beautiful wives and many children, all living

---

*See *The Philosophy of Narayana Guru* and *The Vedānta Sūtras of Narayana Guru* by the present commentator and our commentaries on the other major Upaniṣads as well as *Life's Pilgrimage Through the Gītā*, all published by DK Printworld, New Delhi.

happily in a palace. While dreaming he was woken up by his servant saying sadly, "Your only child is dead by a snakebite." Even on hearing this heartrending news, the father did not care to move from his bed; he just lay there as if day-dreaming. The servant could not understand his state of mind. He said again, "Why do you lie down like this? Your only child is dead!" The brāhmin said, "Your waking me up killed all my beautiful wives and all my children. Here my one child alone is dead. I am not sure, for whose sake should I grieve."

Enlightened masters often remind us of the dream-like nature of life and of the world we are living in. Narayana Guru, for example, says,

> Such altering states are a sort of lengthening dream seen while asleep. As with the one of the ordinary sleep, this dream also ceases immediately. This evanescent (dream-like) nature of life, in the usual course, is not perceived, for the reason that foolish people remain deluded always by their interest in unimportant things. — *Ātmopadeśa Śatakam*. v. 55

We have been discussing so far the dreams of individuated consciousness all of us are familiar with. The universal aspect of consciousness also likewise has its dreams, and these constitute the world of constant change and consist of known and unknown phenomena.

All the dreams seen by a dreamer merge in his being upon waking. Likewise is the world-dream. It also becomes lost in the being of the universal Consciousness called *Brahman* upon its awakening. This waking up is experienced by we humans upon our own awakening from the sleep in which we see the world-dream. This sleep is nothing other than the ignorance of ourselves. Our awakening from this ignorance is in effect the discovery of finding ourselves one with *Brahman*; hence this experience itself is *Brahman*'s waking up.

The consciousness that dreams, whether universal or particular, is brightness (*tejas*) in essence. Though the objective awareness of the waking state also happens in the very same consciousness, in that state, it being brightness in essence remains hidden because our attention then is outwardly oriented. In the inwardly oriented state (*antaḥ-prajñaḥ*), on the other hand, the mind being brightness in essence is felt more directly. Hence the epithet *taijasa* (that which is related to brightness), which pertains to the functional state of consciousness that could be both universal and particular.

Every subjective experience, as stated earlier, is inperceptible and incommunicable to another. The dreams one sees are also personal. Though some of their details could partially be described to another, most of our dreams, and dreams taken together, remain indescribably hidden in the unconscious mind. Still, enjoying such visions happens while dreaming. Hence all dreams and the joy derived from them are solitary in nature and hence it is thought of as *praviviktabhuk* (enjoyer of solitary objects).

All the objects perceived and enjoyed in the waking state are of a gross nature, and are part of the gross external world. Hence the Vaiśvānara aspect of *Ātmā* also, discussed in *mantra* 3, is thought of in traditional Vedānta, as having a gross body (*sthūla-śarīra*), constituted of the five gross elements (*sthūla-bhūtas*). In the dream state, on the other hand, all the objects perceived and enjoyed have their being only as mental images that are subtle in nature. Therefore, the world enjoyed by the Taijasa is subtle (*sūkṣma*), and thus this aspect of *Ātmā* is thought of as having a subtle body (*sūkṣma-śarīra*) comprised of the five basic elements in their subtle form called *tanmātras*. This concept, we should caution, should not mislead us to the idea that the body (*śarīra*) and the Self (*Ātmā*) have separate existences.

In all other respects, the waking experiences and the dream experiences are similar, particularly in respect of the participatory limbs and facets of expression. Hence the epithets *saptāṅgaḥ* (having seven limbs) and *eko na viṁśati-mukhaḥ* (having nineteen facets) are common to both states.

Yet one apparent difference is there between the waking and dream experiences. In the waking state we can continue to live in the same world we lived in previously; we can continue to do things we were doing; and we can continue even to think of the same things we were doing before. But we cannot continue to see the same dream.

But upon scrutiny, our world-picture, like a dream, is one of constant change. The entire world indeed is ever in a state of flux. So we can never live in the same world that we were living in before, because the entire world has changed. The perceiving person also changes likewise. The one who perceives what happens the next moment is not the same person, and the world perceived the next moment is also not the same. This is also true with the dream state.

Verses 5 and 6

यत्र सुप्तो न कंचन कामं कामयते
न कंचन स्वप्नं पश्यति तत् सुषुप्तम्।

सुषुप्तस्थान एकीभूतः
प्रज्ञानघन एवानन्दमयो
ह्यानन्दभुक् चेतोमुखः
प्राज्ञस्तृतीयः पादः ॥

yatra supto na kañcana kāmaṁ kāmayate
na kañcana svapnaṁ paśyati tat suṣuptam ।
suṣuptasthāna ekībhūtaḥ
prajñānaghana evānandamayo
hy ānanda-bhuk cetomukhaḥ
prājñas tṛtīyaḥ pādaḥ ॥

While asleep if one does not desire anything desirable whatsoever and does not see any dream whatsoever, that is the state of deep sleep (*suṣupti*).

Into that sphere of deep sleep become converged the entire mass of cognition. It is unconditioned Happiness in essence, and (itself) enjoys unconditioned Happiness. This state, known as Prājña, having (unconsciously enjoying) mind alone for its facet, is the third quarter.

एष सर्वेश्वर एष सर्वज्ञः
एषोऽन्तर्याम्येष योनिः ।
सर्वस्य प्रभवाप्ययौ हि भूतानाम् ॥

eṣa sarveśvara eṣa sarvajñaḥ
eṣo 'ntar yāmy eṣa yoniḥ ।
sarvasya prabhavāpyayau hi bhūtānām ॥

It is the Supreme controller of everything; It is the all knower; It is the indwelling restrainer of everything; It is the source of everything; It is the emerging and dissolution of all beings.

The third quarter of functional consciousness is named Prājñah which means "the wise one." As a variant form of the word Prajñā, it also means "consciousness."

Prājña's domain of activity or rather actionlessness, is the state of deep sleep (*suṣupta-sthāna*). The prefix *su* in the word *suṣuptam* stands for "in the best way possible," and *suptam* means "in a sleeping state." A *supta* (one who sleeps) could either be seeing dreams or be having a dreamless deep sleep.

This *suṣupta* state is first stated as having no desire for any desirable object. The existence of desirable objects and having a desire for them are relevant only in the waking and dreaming states alone where the enjoyer-enjoyed duality is meaningful. Likewise, having limbs (*aṅga*s) and having several functional facets (*mukha*s) are also only relevant in the waking and dreaming states.

This Prājña, that has deep sleep for its sphere of functioning, is the state of consciousness in which the entire mass of cognition becomes converged. That means, no knowing function takes place in it. All the specific functions of mind that occur variously in the waking and dreaming states become reduced to mere abstract potentials within this Prājña. It is just like that of the potential fire hiding in a match-stick, yet it is capable of growing into a forest-fire, or it is like the possibility to assume the form of all kinds of ornaments, hiding in the gold substance. All the apparent functional states that emanate from this Prājña could be considered its effects; then this state of consciousness is the cause. And the assumed body with which this state remains functional is thought of as the causal body (*kāraṇa-śarīra*). Though considered a body it has no limbs (*aṅga*s), but has one functional facet, namely, that of the unconsciously enjoying mind (*cetomukhaḥ*).

This *cetas* or functional facet of mind is of the nature of unconsciously experiencing (*bhuk*) the unconditioned Happiness-content (*ānanda-maya*) of the Self, and in this sense it is *ānanda-bhuk,* meaning the "enjoyer of Happiness." This experience of Happiness, so stated theoretically, is the actual life experience felt by us in our deep sleep nearly every night. After having a sound sleep we say, "I had a sound sleep; I knew nothing at all." This unconscious enjoyment of a sound sleep, though recalled upon waking, happened really while asleep, not upon waking. But the knowing function then being in a converged seed-like state, the enjoyment took place unknowingly. In that state of enjoyment, the duality between the Happiness-content (*ānanda-maya*) that is enjoyed and the enjoyer of Happiness (*ānanda-bhuk*), also vanishes, because all the cognitive functions of consciousness converge into that causal state.

One's sense of individuality is also a state of awareness. On becoming unconscious, the individual consciousness virtually ceases to be so. It, then, really is neither individual nor universal; it is just consciousness remaining unconscious.

This unconscious Consciousness is what, in its functional states, finds expression as the individual as well as the universal consciousness, as the waking and dreaming states, as the entire subjective and objective worlds. This causal Consciousness, as the indwelling Substance in everything, gross as well as subtle, physical as well as mental, is called *Īśa* in the *Īśa Upaniṣad,* in the sense that It controls or rules everything. The word *īśa* is derived from the root *īś,* meaning "to rule, to be in command" (*īśa-aiśvarye*). *Īśa,* thus, means "the one who rules," "the one who is in control of everything." The suffix *vara* in the word *sarveśvara,* means "the best." Along with the prefix *sarva* meaning "everything," *sarveśvara* means "the best ruler of everything." This unconscious Consciousness unfolds itself functionally as all the experiences of the individual as well as all the worlds experienced universally. The Prājña consciousness in the deep sleep state, thus, is *sarveśvara.*

This Prājña is stated to be *sarvajña* also. *Jñaḥ* means, "one who knows," and *sarvajñaḥ* "one who knows everything." The one who rules everything must be the one who knows everything as well. Everything being the functional manifestation of the one unmanifest Consciousness, all that is manifested should be known to It.

Prājña is also called here *antaryāmin,* one of the well-known epithets of *Brahman* or *Ātman.* It literally means, "the indwelling restrainer." Derived from the verb-root *yam* meaning "to restrain" (*yama uparame*), *yāmin* signifies "one who restrains." *Antaḥ* means "inside" or "inwardly." *Antaryāmin* thus means "the indwelling restrainer." The unconscious-Consciousness-Substance unfolds Itself as a systematized cosmos, not as a chaos. This systematization is made possible by the same Consciousness restraining Its own self-unfolding functions. Thus it is *antaryāmin.*

The same Prājña is also considered the *yoniḥ* of everything. Derived from the root *yu* meaning "to mix" (*yu miśraṇe amiśraṇe ca*), *yoniḥ* means the female genital or womb, and in Vedānta it signifies the seed-like source of everything. Prājña is considered the *yoniḥ* because it is the unconscious-Consciousness-Substance from which everything emanates as its functional modes or *bhānas*, a point to be made clear later in our comments on the next *mantra.* As the potent source of everything, this Consciousness is portrayed by Narayana Guru as follows:

> Latent in it is a primeval creative urge, the original seed that gives birth to everything perceptible forming the world. — *Ātmopadeśa Śatakam* v. 53

The epithets *sarveśvaraḥ, sarvajñaḥ, antaryāmin,* and *yoniḥ* are equally applicable to *Brahman* and *Ātman*. The only factor that differentiates Prājña from *Brahman* is that the former remains unconscious in darkness, with all the potentials to become bright or conscious of everything, whereas *Brahman* is pure effulgence in essence. This *prājña*-consciousness that remains in darkness and dormancy, in its universal dimension, is sometimes referred to as *mūlā-tiraskaraṇī,* as did Narayana Guru in one of his prose-prayers. It literally means, "the causal curtain that makes everything invisible." Rāmānuja's theory, derived from the *Bhāgavata Purāṇa,* is that at the time of the great dissolution, the entire world along with all the souls and their *karma*s become merged into a great darkness and remain dormant in it, hence to re-emerge during the next creation. This could be thought of as somewhat parallel to these ideas.

Finally, Prājña is considered the Reality from which everything emerges (*prabhavaḥ*) and into which everything disappears (*apyayaḥ*). All the waves emerge from the water content of ocean and into it they disappear as well. So too from the unconscious Prājña, hiding as it is within it all the potentials of the conscious functions emerges everything that pertains to the waking and dreaming states, and into it all these disappear. This process continues for ever, creating the never ending appearance of the world and its experience.

This picture, bringing in the idea of *karma*, is portrayed by Narayana Guru as follows:

> Individuated forms, like waves in the ocean, emerge in sequence, and so do they merge. When will this process come to an end? Oh this is nothing but the action (*karma*), in the process of creation, ever unfolding within the ocean of primeval source-Consciousness (*saṁvit*).
>
> — *Ātmopadeśa Śatakam*, verse 56

The *karma*-potential or the potential to be active, latent in the Prājña, called *saṁvit* by Narayana Guru here, when finding expression, appears as all the universal activities of nature like wind blowing, water flowing, fire flaming and the like, and as all individual activities like breathing, heart beating, blood circulating, food getting digested, hands grasping objects, mind thinking, imagining, willing, etc. All the actions, perceived thus, are merely the *karma*-potential of Prājña becoming manifest; thus individuals really have no *karma* of their own. It is only because of the ignorance of this basic truth that people conceive the idea that they are the doers of *karma*s and must eat their kārmic fruits, and then must be reborn in order to finish this eating.

Deep sleep (*suṣuptam*) is the state in which we know nothing, and therefore predicating anything about it is not possible. So it is with *Brahman* or *Ātman*. But Prājña is pure darkness in essence whereas *Brahman* is pure effulgence in essence.

Brahman, as we know, is defined as *sat-cit-ānanda* (Existence-Consciousness-Happiness or Value-sense). *Sat* means "that which exists." *Brahman*, as *sat*, is what really exists as the source of everything appearing to be. This aspect is indicated by the words *eṣa yoniḥ* (it is the source of everything), and *prabhavāpyayau hi bhūtānām* (it is the emerging and dissolution of all beings). Though the source of everything, the apparent emergence and re-mergence of beings remain as nascent possibilities in the purely dark state of deep sleep.

The *cit* (Consciousness) aspect, as is natural with the deep sleep state, becomes converged into a dark point that is potent with all the possibilities of unfolding itself as all mental functions of the waking and dreaming states. The *ānanda* content of *Ātmā,* meanwhile, remains enjoying itself as an object, but it happens unconsciously as the *cit* (Consciousness) or knowing aspect remains non-active. In short, *sat* and *cit* aspects remain dormant in this state of deep sleep and the *ānanda* aspect alone functions which also remains unkown because the *cit* (consciousness) aspect is not active. This non-active state of *cit* is called *ajñāna* (ignorance). For this reason, the consciousness in the deep sleep state is thought to be conditioned by *ajñāna.*

Prājña, acording to Śaṅkara, is called so because, as Vaiśvānara and Taijasa, it knows everything. *Ātmā* really is not known in this state nor is anything else perceived. Though the *ānanda*-content is known, it happens when veiled by ignorance or not-knowing, and hence remains unknown. The happiness felt in this state, for this reason, is not considered *ānanda-svarūpa-darśana* (the intuitive perception of the *ānanda*-content of *Ātman*), but merely as *ānanda-pracurimā* (the abundance of happiness). The *ānanda* experienced in deep sleep really is the absence of all pains and pleasures because *cit* is non-functional in that state.

An ignorance, as we have seen, envelopes the state of deep sleep. This ignorance could be conceived as having two facets; one, knowing something wrongly (*anyathā-grahaṇa*), and two, not knowing (*agrahaṇa*). While both these facets of ignorance are present in the waking and dreaming states, the latter kind alone is present in deep sleep.

The state of deep sleep, in other words, has no transactional (*vyāvahārika*) function of consciousness, whereas in the two other states consciousness functions transactionally. To put the same using a visual-structural language, the functions of consciousness in the *Jāgarita* and *svapna* states have a horizontal status where the enjoyer-enjoyed duality is meaningful. The *suṣupti* state, on the other hand, has a vertical dimension. As all that is distinguishable becomes converged into the oneness of the all-engulfing darkness, this state could well be placed at the negative (–) pole of the vertical axis. (See the figure that forms part of our comments on the next *mantra*). Then the waking state has its place at the plus (+) pole of the horizontal axis, for it is objective in status; and the dreaming state is at the negative (–) pole because it is a subjective experience. The fourth state (*turīya*), to be portrayed in the next *mantra*, could then be placed at the positive (+) pole of the vertical axis, for it is a state or rather a non-state, in which everything becomes merged in the brightness of self-awareness. *Suṣupti* (deep sleep), on the other hand, is the state of consciousness in which all differentiations vanish in the utter darkness of unconsciousness.

Verse 7

नान्तः प्रज्ञं न बहिःप्रज्ञम्
नोभयतः प्रज्ञं न प्रज्ञानघनम्
न प्रज्ञं नाप्रज्ञम् ।

अदृष्टमव्यवहार्यमग्राह्यम्
अलक्षणमचिन्त्यमव्यपदेश्यम्
एकात्मप्रत्ययसारम्
प्रपञ्चोपशमं शान्तं शिवमद्वैतम्
चतुर्थं मन्यन्ते स आत्मा स विज्ञेयः ॥

nāntaḥ-prajñaṁ na bahiḥ-prajñam
nobhayataḥ prajñaṁ na prajñānaghanam
na prajñaṁ nāprajñam ।
adṛṣṭam avyavahāryam agrāhyam
alakṣaṇam acintyam avyapadeśyam
ekātma-pratyaya-sāram
prapañcopaśamaṁ śāntaṁ śivam advaitam
caturthaṁ manyante sa ātmā sa vijñeyaḥ ॥

Not cognized and cognizing inwardly, not cognized and cognizing outwardly, not cognized and cognizing bothwise, not the mass of cognition, not cognizable, not non-cognizable, unseen, with which there can be no interacting, ungraspable, having no distinctive mark, unthinkable, unnameable, the fourth is thought to be. It, in essential content, is the experience of the beingness of the one Self, wherein the entire phenomenal world ceases to be, is perfect tranquillity, the most auspicious and the non-dual. It is the Self. (It is oneself.) It is to be specifically known.

This seventh *mantra* portrays the fourth (*caturtha*) state of consciousness. The *Bṛhadāraṇyaka Upaniṣad* (5.14.3) says "the fourth" is also called *turīya*. This experiential state transcends the duality of the universal and the particular. What this *mantra* pictures as "the fourth" is stated to be none other than *Ātmā* (the Self or oneself) at the end of the *mantra*. Hence all that is stated as helpful to meditate on the *turīya* also helps one to meditate on the Self or oneself.

The Self (*Ātmā*), as the metaphysical, abstract and intuitively experienced Reality, is to be meditated on as stated in this *mantra*. Then it is to be understood as different from the other three states. But upon realizing the Self, its transparency reveals that the other three quarters or states have no existence apart from *Ātmā;* these states exist only as Its shining functional manifestations (*bhānas*). *Ātmā* is a word translatable as "the self" as well as "oneself." Hence, whatever is stated here about *Ātmā* is true with oneself also, because oneself really is none other than *Ātmā.*

First it is stated that the *turīya* or the true *Ātmā* does not cognize and is not cognized inwardly (*na antaḥ-prajñaḥ*). To be cognitive as we know is the most basic function of *ātmā.* But the cognition of *ātmā,* in its real *turīya* state, is an all-engulfing effulgent experience in which the cognizer becomes merged. Therfore, for the cognizer to state that it is such and such is not possible. All such possible statements are examined here one by one and each is rejected as invalid.

Of these negating statements, the first is *na antaḥ-prajñaḥ* (not cognized and cognizing inwardly). To be inwardly cognitive, as was noted earlier in *mantra* 4, is a function of the dreaming state. *Turīya* is different from that.

The opposite possibility of this is, to be *bahiḥ-prajñaḥ* (outwardly cognized and cognizing). To be so is natural with the waking state, as seen in *mantra* 3. *Turīya* must also necessarily be different from that.

Then the other possibility is, to be cognized and cognizing both inwardly and outwardly. For such a function to take place in consciousness is not natural to it, the knowing function has either to be one or the other. The change from one state to the other could take place as quickly as the fluttering of a butterfly's wings. Still the mind does not function as both simultaneously.

To be *prajñāna-ghana* (pure consciousness in essence) is natural with the deep sleep state as was seen in *mantra* 5. *Turīya* is different from that state as well.

In effect, *turīya* is not a state of consciousness which we can say something about. What we are familar with as knowledge has to pertain to one of the three states already examined. Anything not known in the three states is therefore to be considered beyond the bounds of knowledge and thus is "not cognizable" (*na prājña*).

But, being the experiential effulgence of pure Consciousness, it is meaningless to say that it is "not cognizable." As we are well aware, *turīya* marks the ultimate limit of knowing, where everything specific including the knower becomes merged in the effulgence of unconditioned Consciousness. Therefore it is not "non-cognizable" (*na aprājña*) either.

Seeing, interacting with, and grasping are possible only with objects. Being no object, *turīya* is unseen (*adṛṣṭa*) with which there can be no interacting (*avyavahārya*), and it is also ungraspable (*agrāhya*).

Lakṣaṇa means the defining qualities of something. Not having any such qualities, *turīya* is *alakṣaṇa* (having no distinctive mark).

Thinking, as we know, is possible only with something that has distinguishing features, whether objectively perceived or subjectively conceived. No such distinguishing feature can be attributed to *turīya*. Can't we then think of it as qualityless? Then the absence of quality becomes itself a distinguishing feature. In short, *tirīya* is attributeless and thus is unthinkable (*acintya*).

It is also innameable (*avyapadeśya*). Naming is done when taking into account the characteristics of what is named. The world famous *Tao Te Ching* of Lao Tsu begins with the sweeping statement, "The Tao that can be expressed is not the eternal Tao. The name that can be defined is not the unchanging name." The same is true with *turīya*. We know *turīya* is stated to be *Ātman* at the end of the *mantra*. Is not *Ātman* a name? Is not *Brahman* a name? Is not *turīya* itself a name? *Brahman* really is not a name, it shows one of the functional aspects of what ultimately exists as "that which grows incessantly," and *Ātmā* also, likewise, means, "that which pervades the being of everything," and *turīya* merely means "the fourth." None of these, therefore, is to be treated as a name. Naming is possible only with something perceivable or conceivable. *Turīya* is not such; it simply is an inner experience of transparency.

Everything stated so far about *turīya* is a sort of negative definition. That means, these statements say only what it is not, not what it really is. *Turīya* being indefinable, its only possible definition can be of a negative nature. So with *Ātmā* also. The *Bṛhadāraṇyaka Upaniṣad* also, when it comes to defining *Ātmā*, resorts to the same method as it repeatedy says "*neti neti*" (not thus, not thus). (*Bṛhadāraṇyaka Upaniṣad* 2.3.6, 3.9.26). Furthermore, almost all introductory textbooks of Vedānta, when trying to clarify what *Ātmā* is, resort to the device of describing in detail, all that constitutes the non-self (*anātmā*) followed by saying, that which is not this non-self is the Self. Nonetheless, a positive definition of *Ātmā* is given by Narayana Guru as follows:

> That which is conscious of itself even when in darkness is the *Ātmā*. — *Ātmopadeśa Śatakam*, v. 27

Similarly, the *turīya* also, traditionally considered indefinable, is given a positive definition, while not losing its touch of mystical experience, by Narayana Guru at the very next verse as follows:

> Attainning to clarity of the one bottomless and topless (unconditioned pure Consciousness) from bottom to top with full transparence, is to be understood as *turīya* consciousness. Never known it is to the inert aspect of being, nor is it known as pertaining to the realm where thinking and communicating hold good; be fully aware! — *Ātmopadeśa Śatakam*, v. 28

Of course, a few positive elements rather pertaining to the experiential aspect than forming any definition, is given at the end of the *mantra*. It reads:

> It merely is the one essential content of self-experience wherein the entire phenomenal world ceases to be, is perfect tranquility, is the most auspicious, and the non-dual.

After stating that this *turīya* is itself the real *Ātmā*, it says *sa vijñeyaḥ* (It is to be specifically known). *Njeyaḥ* means "that which is to be known," and *vjñeyaḥ*, "that which is to be specifically known." Is it possible to know *turīya* or *Ātmā* specifically? No. But *vijñāna* (specific wisdom), as elaborated in chapter VII of the *Bhagavad Gītā*, means, the inner clarity of perceiving the one invisible *Ātmā* in all that is specifically experienced. For example, taste is the distinguishing quality of water. Water and its quality taste are thus to be visualized as the one qualityless *Ātmā* having become manifest with qualities. Śrī Kṛṣṇa, in the *Bhagavad Gītā* says *"raso 'ham apsu kaunteya"* (O Arjuna, the quality of taste in water is myself). In other words, when you enjoy the taste of water you should see the one *Ātmā* alone manifesting in it. Such a clarity enables you to perceive *Ātmā* alone in everything, and this perception is known as *vijñāna,* and that which is to be known as *vijñāna* is *vijñeya.* In other words, *Ātmā* as well as *turīya* is not to be understood specifically as such and such, but the attributeless *Ātmā* or *turīya* is to be incessantly perceived in every specific experience we have in life. Such is the way the words *"sa vijñeyaḥ"* (It is to be specifically known) are to be construed.

So far we have been trying to state verbally what the four quarters of *Ātmā* signify. *Ātmā* being the one Reality that fleetingly manifests as all phenomenal appearances, nothing is outside its ambit. All that we have understood as pertaining to the waking, dreaming and deep sleep states are but various states in which the one *Ātmā* finds self-expression. Therefore the words *sa Ātmā sa vijñeyaḥ* could be construed as, meaning, "This *turīya* is the *Ātmā* and it is to be perceived in all its specific manifest forms." Or these words could be understood as signifying, "Such is the *Ātmā* and It is to be perceived in all specific manifest forms like the three states already examined."

All these could well be comprehended with the help of a Cartesian diagram, a method devised by the French philosopher Rene Descartes:

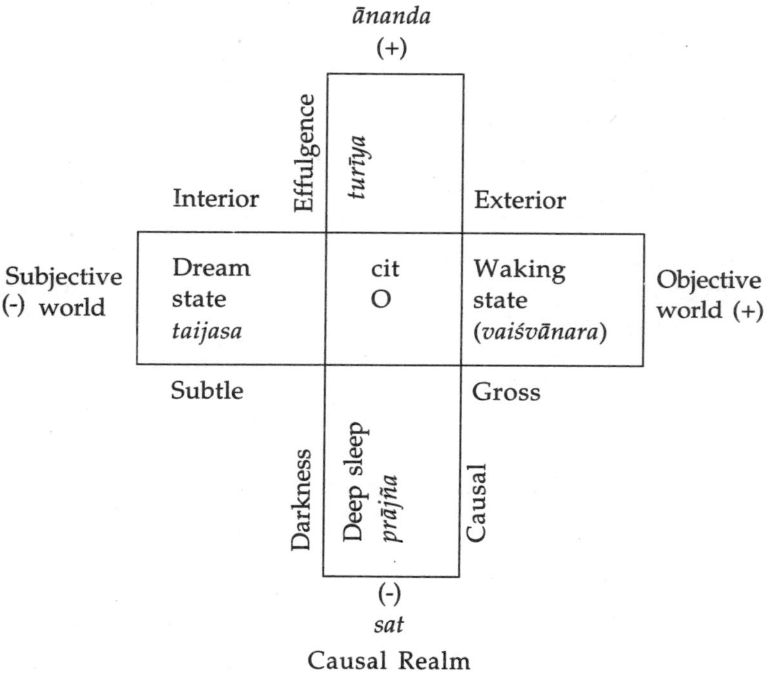

Notes: The horizontal axis represents the transactional world (*vyāvahārika-loka*). It is the realm of fleeting appearances. The vertical axis stands for the ultimate and eternal Reality (*pāramārthika-satya*), which in its abstract state is *sat-cit-ānanda* in essence.

Both the axes have their respective plus and minus poles. The positive pole of the horizontal axis represents the waking state, examined in *mantra* 3 of this Upaniṣad. It is the sphere of activities of *Vaiśvānara*, the enjoyer of gross and external objects. This positive side altogether represents the objective, external world.

The minus pole of the horizontal axis stands for the dream state examined in *mantra* 4. It is the sphere of activities of *Taijasa*, the enjoyer of the solitary, subjective world. This pole, in all its aspects, signifies the subjective, internal world.

The negative pole of the vertical axis represents the deep sleep state (*suṣupti*), the sphere of activities of *Prājña*. It is the non-active consciousness-Reality in its causal state. It becomes horizontalized as effects forming the subjective and objective experiences. Everything specific, in this state, becomes merged into the utter darkness of the causal Substance. This pole thus represents the *sat* aspect of *saccidānanda.*

The positive pole of the vertical axis represents the transcendental experience of *turīya.* Everything specific, in this state, becomes merged in the pure effulgence of Self-realization. The transcendental *ānanda* of *saccidānanda* could be seen placed at this pole.

The neutral *O* point which is neither vertical nor horizontal, neither positive nor negative, represents non-duality. Of *saccidānanda,* the *cit* aspect could be seen at this neutral point. The *cit,* functionally, finds expression both as the subjective (–) and objective (+) experiences.

Ātmā, both in the *suṣupti* and *turīya* states, really experiences its own *ānanda* (Happiness)-content. The only difference is that this *ānanda*-experience, in the former state, happens unknowingly in *Ātmā*'s deepest and darkest realms, whereas in the latter state, the *ānanda*-content of *Ātmā* is directly experienced by *Ātmā* as a fully enlightened experience of all-filling brightness.

Interlude

It is the function of consciousness in its four states described so far that creates, from itself, the respective worlds of experience. Of these experiential worlds, the one familier to the waking state (*Jāgarita*) is alone recognized to be real according to modern science, whereas the worlds familiar to the four states are admitted as real by Vedānta. Of these four levels of the world, only the first two — the ones experienced in waking and dreaming states — are discernible and describable; all the discernible details in the other two remain merged in their darkness and brightness respectively.

The external world of objects; the internal world of ideas, imaginations and dreams; the idealess, imaginationless and dreamless deep sleep where the subjective and objective worlds become merged in the utter darkness of ignorance; the transcendental awareness in which the subjective and objective worlds become lost in the all-engulfing effulgence — all these experiences and the concerned worlds experienced are but various functional modes of Consciousness. These modes of consciousness are known as *bhānas*, meaning the shining manifest forms. The four states (*avasthās*) conceived in the *Māṇḍūkya Upaniṣad*, therefore, are thought of as four *bhānas* of Consciousness by Narayana Guru in the *Bhāna-darśanam* (Vision of Reality through *bhāna*) of his *Darśana-mālā* (Garland of Visions). The Guru thus differentiates *sthūla-bhāna* (gross manifestation of consciousness), *sūkṣma-bhāna* (subtle manifestation of consciousness), *kāraṇa-bhāna* (causal manifestation of consciousness) and *turīya-bhāna* (the fourth manifestation of consciousness). Each such *bhāna* has its own *bhānāśraya* (that on which the manifestation of consciousness depends) as well. These *bhānas* have their own respective generic and specific aspects. To quote the Guru's own words:

antar bahirvad āsīnam
sadā bhramara-cañcalam ।
bhānam dvidhaiva sāmānyam
viśeṣa iti bhidyate ॥1॥

Presenting itself as existing.
Both inside as subjects
And outside as objects,
And also fluttering constantly like a bee,
The manifestation of Consciousness
Is divisible into two kinds:
Generic and specific.

Both the objectively experienced worlds and the subjectively experienced knowldge of the worlds are thus nothing other than the different *bhāna*s of one Consciousness or *Ātmā.*

sthūlam sūkṣmam kāraṇam ca
tūryam cedi caturvidham ।
bhānāśrayam hi tan nāma
bhānasyāpy upacaryate ॥2॥

That on which the manifestation
Of Consciousness depends,
Is of four kinds:
Gross, subtle, causal and *turīya* (the fourth).
The very same division is applicable
To the manifestation of Consciousness as well.

dṛśyatām iha kāyo 'ham
ghaṭo 'yam iti dṛśyate ।
sthūlam āśṛtya yad bhānam
sthūlam tad iti manyate ॥3॥

That manifestation of Consciousness
Which depends on gross aspects
And finds expression as
Experiences like, "Look here,
I am the body," "This is a pot,"
Is considered the gross (*sthūla*).

atra kāyo ghaṭa iti
bhānam yat tad viśiṣyate ।
tathāham ayam iti yat
sāmānyam iti ca smṛtam ॥4॥

Of such instances,
The manifestation of Consciousness.
That assumes the forms such as
"I" and "This" is to be known
As the generic gross manifestation,
And similarly, that which assumes
The forms such as "the body" and "the pot"
Is specific gross manifestation.

A clarification on what the generic (*sāmānya*) and specific (*viśeṣa*) *bhāna*s, are, it seems, is needed.

Take, for example, the case of the gross experience, "This is a pot." This statement has in it two parts: "This", and "is a pot." Suppose someone, referring to an object, simply says, "This." Such a statement impresses no clear idea upon our mind; it simply makes the impression that something is going to be said about something. Furthermore, the pronoun "This" could be used to denote anything perceived. Therefore, the impression created on hearing the word "This" is of a generic nature. This generic and vague idea gains specificity and clarity as the words "is a pot" are added. Therefore "is a pot" is considered the specific gross manifestation of Consciousness (*viśeṣa-sthūla-bhāna*), whereas "this" is the generic gross manifestation of Consciousness (*sāmānya-sthūla-bhāna*). The generic and specific aspects of the other three *bhāna*s are to be understood in the same way.

indriyāṇi mano buddhī
viṣayāḥ pañca-vāyavaḥ ।
bhāsyante yena tat sūkṣmam
asya sūkṣmāśrayatvataḥ ॥5॥

That owing to which
The senses, mind, intellect
And their corresponding objects
As well as the five vital airs,
Appear manifestly, is known as
The subtle (*sūkṣma*) manifestation of Consciousness.
For the reason of its
Dependence on subtle factors.

ajño 'ham iti yad bhānam
tat kāraṇam udāhṛtam ।
atrāham iti sāmānyam
viśeṣo 'jña iti sphurat ॥6॥

The manifestation of Consciousness
In the form "I am ignorant"
Is said to be causal (*kāraṇa*).
Of it the "I"-part is generic,
And the "am ignorant"-part is specific.

aham brahmeti yad bhānam
tat turyaṁ iti śaṁsyate ।
sāmānyam aham ity aṁśo
brahmety atra viśiṣyate ॥7॥

The manifestation of Consciousness
Owing to which one experiences,

"I am *Brahman,*"
Is glorified as *turīya* (the fourth).
Of it, the "I"-part is generic
And the "am *Brahman*"-part, specific.

yatra bhānam tatra bhāṣyam
bhānam yatra na tatra na ।
bhāsyam ity anvayenāpi
vyatirekeṇa bodhyate ॥8 ॥

Wherever manifestation of
Consciousness takes place,
There appears the object made manifest as well;
And wherever manifestation of
Consciousness does not take place,
There appears no manifest form either.
Certitude is attained thus by the method
Of agreement and difference.

It is to be particularly noted here that even the *turīya* is treated by the Guru as a *bhāna* or a manifest form of Consciousness, that means, a conditioned state of Consciousness, because to the extent we conceive an idea about *turīya,* it is a conditioned state, and thus a *bhāna.* The real unconditioned *Ātmā* can never be known as an object, as we can know of something.

Though *Ātmā* is thus never known as an object, that which is perceived by *Ātmā* is what gains the status of being an object of knowledge. To quote the Guru's own words:

yathā dr̥g dr̥śam ātmānam
svayam ātmā na paśyati ।
ato no bhāṣyate hy ātmā
yam paśyati sa bhāṣyate ॥9 ॥

The eye does not see itself.
So too *Ātmā* does not perceive itself.
Ātmā, therefore, is no object
Of the knowing function of Consciousness.
Whatever *Ātmā* perceives is
What becomes manifest as objects.

Nothing really can be predicated of the real non-dual *Ātmā* as made explicit by the Guru:

yad bhāsyate tad adhyastam
anadhyastam na bhāṣyate ।
yad adhyastam tad asad
apy anadhyastam śad eva tat ॥10 ॥

That which is made manifest
By the knowing function of Consciousness
Is superimposed.
That which is not superimposed
Never becomes an object
Of the knowing function of Consciousness.
That which is superimposed
Is unreal.
That which is not superimposed is
The *sat* which alone is "That."

Readers are advised to go through the detailed analysis of the *Bhāna-darśanam* we have made in chapter 11 of *The Philosophy of Narayana Guru* and chapter IV of the *Garland of Visions* (both published by D.K. Printworld).

Mantras 3 to 7 so far, examined the *abhidheya* side (that which is denoted) of Reality; that is to say, the *abhidheya* side is "everything" (*sarvam*) which is equated to *Brahman,* and then equated to *Ātman.* This *Ātman* is nothing but unconditioned Consciousness in essence. Finally, this pure

Consciousness is analysed in the Upaniṣad in order to have a clear awareness of *Ātman, Brahman* and *sarvam*. The remaining *mantras* of the Upaniṣad concentrate on the *abhidhāna* (denotation) side, that means, the *auṁ* side that linguistically signifies the above mentioned *abhidheya*. The two sides, as *mantra* 8 clearly states, are such that each state of Consciousness or quarter (*pāda*) on the one side is equatable to each constituent letter (*mātrā*) of the symbol *auṁ* on the other. That means, both sides are of equal status.

Really neither the *abhidheya* side nor the *abhidhāna* side is the Real. The ultimate Reality is what exists between these two opposite sides. It is like the real value-content in a coin that exists between its two sides. This Reality is necessarily left unstated because it is ineffable. But this Reality is meant to be intuitively perceived and realized by the seeker on his own. This kind of search for the unstated Reality is really the essential content of all spiritual enquiry and is called *sādhanā*. This way of arriving at the realization of what is real within oneself is known as *yoga-buddhi* in India, and as dialectics in the West.

Verse 8

सोयमात्माध्यक्षरमोंकारोऽधिमात्रम्
पादा मात्रा मात्राश्च पादा
अकार उकारो मकार इति ॥

soyam ātmādhyakṣaram oṁkārodhimātram
pādā mātrā mātrāśca pādā
akāra ukāro makāra iti ॥

This Self, being such, seen based on syllables, is *auṁ*. In regard to the elements (that form *auṁ*), the quarters are the elements, and the elements are the quarters.

These elements are the letters *A*, *U* and *Ṁ*.

This *Ātmā* that was portrayed in *mantra*s 3 to 7 is the Reality here to be denoted in the world of communication. In the world of linguistic symbols, as was stated in the very first *mantra, Ātma* is denoted by the syllable *auṁ*, and hence the present *mantra* equates the two. *Adhyakṣaram* (*adhi+akṣaram*) is the word used here in the place of *abhidhāna* (denotation). *Akṣaram* means a syllable or linguistic symbol, and the prefix *adhi* stands for "making it the basis." That means, *Ātmā,* in the context of linguistic symbols, is equatable to *auṁ*.

Ātmā, as we know, is unconditioned Consciousness in essence, though It never remains in an unconditioned state in actuality. These conditioned or functional states were described from *mantra*s 3 to 7, and each such conditioned state was considered as a quarter of *Ātmā.* Each quarter is here represented by one of the four constituent elements (*mātrā*s) of *auṁ*, namely *A, U, Ṁ* and the silence or *amātrā* (non-element) that follows. Though this *amātrā* is not mentioned here in the present *mantra,* the concluding *mantra* (12) of the Upaniṣad exclusively portrays it. A complete parity is thus seen between the *abhidheya* and the *abhidhāna* aspects of *Ātmā.*

Verse 9

जागरितस्थानो वैश्वानरोऽकारः
प्रथमा मात्रा आप्तेरादिमत्वाद्वा
आप्नोति ह वै सर्वान् कामान्
आदिश्च भवति य एवं वेद ॥

jāgarita-sthāno vaiśvānaro 'kāraḥ
prathamā mātrā āpter ādimatvād vā

> *āpnoti ha vai sarvān kāmān*
> *ādiś ca bhavati ya evaṁ veda* ॥
>
> The first element (*mātrā*), the letter *A*, is *Vaiśvānara* whose sphere of activity is the waking state, because of its all pervasiveness (*āpnoti*) or because it is the first and the pre-eminent (*ādimat*). He who knows thus feels the satisfaction of having fulfilled all desires, and he becomes pre-emiment.

This *mantra* equates the first quarter of *Ātmā, Vaiśvānara* whose sphere of activity is the waking state, with the letter *A*, the first constituent element of the syllable *auṁ*. Consciousness in the waking state, as we know, opens itself outwards. The sound we can utter with our mouth fully open is "*A*." This could be one of the reasons for equating *Vaiśvānara* with the letter *A*, though this is not mentioned openly in the *mantra*.

Two are the reasons stated in the *mantra* for such an equation. The first is, "because of its all-pervasiveness" (*āpteḥ*). Even though consciousness functions in states categorizable as the four quarters, such a categorization is done by us in our waking state, and no such examining is possible in the other three states. Therefore we could very well say, the waking state thoroughly pervades the other states also. Similarly each letter in the language of any alphabet is pronounced with the mouth opened differently. *A* being the letter utterable with the mouth fully open, we could rightly claim, the sound "*A*" pervades throughout the other alphabetic sounds of letters when pronounced. Thus the two are equitable.

The other reason stated for equating *Vaiśvānara* with *A* is "because it is the first and pre-eminent (*ādimatvāt*)." The first state that comes to our attention when we think of the functional states of consciousness is that of waking. It is in the waking state that this very categorization of consciousness is done, and by which the other states are conceived, with our understanding of the waking state as a norm or measuring rod. Hence pre-eminence is given to the waking state. The letter *A* also has its pre-eminence in that it is the first letter of the alphabet of most of the world's languages. The *Bhagavad Gītā* also admits that among letters, *A* could be meditated upon as representing *Brahman* or *Ātman*. Thus the two sides, *Vaiśvānara* and the letter *A* are equatable.

Perceiving *Vaiśvānara*, the named, of the waking state (*Jāgarita*) and the naming element *A*, as forming the pair of opposites, like the two opposite sides of a coin, enables us to reach the non-dualistic vision relevant at this level of understanding consciousness.

Mantras 9 to 12 end by pronouncing what the ultimate benefit of having the understanding stated in each is. Such a pronouncement, very often seen in scriptural contexts, is known as *phalaśruti* (scriptural statement of the benefit of the teaching just given).

Two benefits are stated here: one, becoming satisfied of having fulfilled all one's desires, and two, becoming pre-eminent. Both are worldly values felt to be meaningful in the waking state, but are really meant to be understood as pertaining to the wisdom context.

To be in contact with external objects is the basic function of consciousness in the waking state. Each such object gives us a feeling that could be either pleasant (*iṣṭa*), unpleasant (*aniṣṭa*) or arousing indifference (*udāsīna*).

Becoming satisfied with the pleasure experienced from objects is the most basic value cherished in the waking state by all. Here the *mantra* says, one who has a proper understanding of *Vaiśvānara* as forming a quarter of the functional domain of consciousness equated to the letter *A*, experiences the benefit of having this worldly value fully satisfied.

This does not mean that those who wish to enjoy worldly pleasures to the utmost may resort to the means of having this dialectical understanding. On the other hand, this understanding enables one to intuitively perceive *Ātmā*'s full glory with *Vaiśvānara* as a means. This perception of *Ātmā* makes one, instead of becoming infatuated with pleasurable objects, detatched from pleasurable objects and find the real, eternal joy of perceiving *Ātmā* as oneself, with the waking state or *Vaiśvānara* as a means of approach. One then becomes free of all desire for pleasurable objects. No one in actual life can really experience the happiness of having fulfilled all desires, because fulfilling one desire is followed by the desire for another, and this goes on endlessly. On the other hand, the one who remains desireless, a state attained by the dialectical understanding portrayed here, ever remains in the satisfaction of having no desire remaining unfulfilled. The reference, therefore, in the *mantra* to "the satisfaction of having fulfilled all desires" is to be understood in this sense.

Similarly, fame (*kīrti*) is a noble worldly value cherished by all. In deliberate efforts, some spend prodigious amounts of money in order to create the impression that they are persons of repute. This kind of fame is much different from the one that comes undesired, and comes because they are wise men (*jñānins*). The understanding of the function of consciousness and its dialectical relationship with the world of words is what makes them really wise. The pre-eminence attained through this wisdom is what the word *ādiḥ* (the state of being pre-eminent and first) signifies in this *mantra.*

Verse 10

स्वप्नस्थानस्तैजस
उकारो द्वितीया मात्रा
उत्कर्षाद्भयत्वाद्वा
उत्कर्षति ह वै ज्ञानसन्ततिं
समानश्च भवति
नास्याब्रह्मविद्कुले भवति
य एवं वेद ॥

svapna-sthānas taijasa
ukāro dvitīyā mātrā
utkarṣād ubhayatvād vā
utkarṣati ha vai jñāna-santatiṁ
samānaśca bhavati
nāsyābrahmanvid kule bhavati
ya evaṁ veda ॥

The second element (*mātrā*), the letter *U*, is *Taijasa* whose sphere of activity is the dreaming state, because of its upliftedness (*utkarṣa*) or because it touches both ends (*ubhayatva*). He who knows thus uplifts the lineage of wisdom; he finds himself in a common ground; into his family line is born no one who is not a *Brahman*-knower.

Taijasa (literally, "the bright one"), as we know, is the functional state of *Ātmā* in which we dream. This part of *abhidheya* is equated here to the letter *U*, the second constituent element (*mātrā*) of the syllable *auṁ*, the *abhidhāna*.

Two reasons are stated here for this equating. One is its being uplifted (*utkarṣa*). If we conceive of the waking state in which we enjoy external objects, to touch the down-to-earth level of existence, then the dreaming state pertains to a subtler level. Attaining subtlety is always considered a process of ascending or going upwards in thought. Together, the dreaming state and *taijasa* thus occupy a realm higher than the waking state and *Vaiśvānara.* We also feel freer to choose what to perceive and what not to in the waking state. No such freedom of choice is possible in the dreams. The more we ascend into the subtler levels of thinking, the less control we have in those realms. At the attainment of the final stage of this subtlety or upliftment, the one who chooses becomes completely lost in the being of what is chosen. *Taijasa* simply marks the initial stage of this upliftment.

This upliftment could be seen in the case of the letter *U* also, which is to be uttered with the mouth half open or half closed. The letter *U*, leaving behind the grossness of the letter *A*, thus rises up to a subtler level of sound utterance. Being uplifted to a subtler level thus happens in respect of *Taijasa* as well as the letter *U*. In this sense, the two are equatable.

The other reason stated why these two are equated is that both have characteristics of the waking state and the sleeping state (*ubhayatva*). The dream state, as was noted earlier, is a functional mode in which consciousness oscillates between fully waking and fully deep sleep states.

Dreams have thus the characteristic experiences known in the waking state as well as that of sleep. Dreams, as all of us know, are seen while we are asleep. The peculiarities of the sleeping state are thus natural with dreams. Yet we see in our mental horizon many specifiable things in dreams as we do in our waking state, though we do not have any control over these. The function of *Taijasa* thus has characteristics peculiar to both the waking and sleeping states.

The ultimate benefit of realizing the oneness of *Taijasa* and the letter *U* is also two-sided. One side results in finding oneself as *samāna;* while the other side ensures that no one is born into one's lineage who is not a *Brahman*-knower (*brahmavit*).

The word *samāna,* though rendered here as"finding oneself in the common ground" literally means "equal," or "neutral" as well as "being respected by all." The one who is enlightened of the neutral position of *Taijasa* as equatable with *U,* thinks of all life as a prolonged dream, and all vagaries of life are then perceived with a sense of equanimity, finding one's stand firm in neutrality. Such a person constantly feels an undisturbed peace in life which easily radiates to everyone around. The result is that all those around respect that person, and in that sense also he becomes *samāna.*

In the two remaining *mantra*s we will come across still higher levels of the *Brahman*-wisdom that reach the levels of realization. The present *Brahman*-knower could therefore be understood as pertaining to a conceptual order. Understanding oneself as *Brahman* is more relevant in this context than *experiencing* it. Construing such a meaning would be more in line with the dreaming state we are dealing with in the present *mantra*, for all conceptualizations are a sort of dreaming. The state of being a *Brahmavit* is defined by Narayana Guru as follows:

> *Brahmavit* is the one who,
> Having burned down everything
> In the fire of wisdom,
> Finds himself in *Brahman*.
> He performs actions in confornity with
> The prescribed rules of conduct,
> Aiming at the good of the *world*.
>
> — *Darśana-mālā*, X.5.

Verse 11

सुषुप्तस्थानः प्राज्ञो मकारस्तृतीया मात्रा
मितेरपीतेर्वा मिनोति ह वा
इदं सर्वमपीतिश्च भवति
य एवं वेद ॥

suṣupta-sthānaḥ prājño
makāras tr̥tīyā mātrā
miter apīter vā minoti ha va
idam sarvam apītiśca bhavati
ya evam veda ॥

The third element (*mātrā*), the letter *Ṁ*, is *Prājña* whose sphere of activity is deep sleep, because of being the measure or because of the merging (of everything specific). He who knows thus measures everything here (as himself) or (everything here) merges (in himself).

This *mantra* equates *Prājña,* whose sphere of activity is deep sleep, with the letter *Ṁ* the third constituent element of the syllable *aum̐*. The reasons for doing so are two: one, because both *Prājña* and *Ṁ* function as a measure or norm. As was noticed earlier, *Prājña* is the causal Consciousness that unfolds itself as both the subjective (dream) and objective (waking) worlds. Cause, we know, is the measure with which all the effects are measured, as are all waves understood as the forms emerging in the causal water; or as ornaments are understood in terms of gold. Likewise, all the worlds and all the specific entities in them are measured as manifest forms of the one causal Consciousness or *Prājña*. So too, the variant forms of the humming pronouncement of "*Ṁ*" pervade throughout the verbal forms, and thus *Ṁ* serves somewhat like a measure within the realm of uttered sounds.

Prājña is the state of consciousness in which everything specific becomes dissolved to find its oneness (*apītiḥ*), as we have noticed earlier in *mantra* 5. Likewise, the humming of "*Ṁ*" is the sound in which all the specifiable sounds become dissolved to find their oneness. Therefore, the two, *Prājña* and the sound "*Ṁ*" are equatable.

The benefit of having a proper understanding of this oneness of *Prājña* and the sound "*Ṁ*" is also two pronged. On the one side, it is felt that oneself or the Self (*Ātmā*) is the measure of everything. That means, one experiences the joy of perceiving everything in terms of oneself, and thus the Happiness of seeing everything as not different from oneself. On the other side he feels everything merges in himself, finding himself or the Self alone existing. Seeing oneself in everything and seeing everything merging in the being of oneself, in fact, are merely two facets of one non-dualistic experience.

Verse 12

अमात्रश्चतुर्थोऽव्यवहार्यः
प्रपञ्चोपशमः शिवोऽद्वैत ।
एवमोंकार आत्मैव
संविशत्यात्मनात्मानं
य एवं वेद य एवं वेद ॥

amātraś caturtho 'vyavahāryaḥ
prapañcopaśamaḥ śivo 'dvaita
evam oṁkāra ātmaiva
saṁviśaty ātmanātmānaṁ
ya evaṁ veda ya evam veda ॥

The fourth is the non-element (*amātrā*) with which there can be no interacting, wherein the entire phenomenal world ceases to be. It is the most auspicious and the non-dual. The sound *auṁ* thus is *Ātmā* indeed. He who knows thus enters *Ātmā* by himself; Yes, he who knows thus.

The fourth state or non-state *turīya* is represented in the syllable *auṁ* by the silence with which the uttering of "*auṁ*" ends. This silence is not an element as *A*, *U*, and *Ṁ* are, and hence it is treated as a non-element (*amātrā*). As nothing can be predicated of *turīya*, so too nothing can be said about the equating of it with silence.

This equating marks the final stage of spiritual attainment conceived in all the Upaniṣads. That is, the seeker enters the ultimate Reality or *Ātmā* and experientally becomes lost in *Ātmā*.

Thus, we have taken into account *Ātmā* as a whole and also its four quarters. It is equatable to *auṁ* constituted of the three elements *A*, *U*, and *Ṁ* and the non-element or silence.

The Upaniṣad thus explicates a comprehensive view of

Ātmā or *Brahman* ranging from a semantic perspective to pinpointing the ultimate value of having this vision. One of the peculiarities noticeable in this Upaniṣad is that, in line with the fourfold division of *Ātmā* as well as *auṁ*, the experience of having this vision is also stated to have four stages where each level of understanding has its own value experience. These four stages could well be put in vertical order as shown below. The stage of *mantra* 9 has a place in touching the earth or the worldly level, and that of *mantra* 12 can be placed at the highest level where the mystical union of the seeker with what he seeks, *Ātmā*, is fully realized.

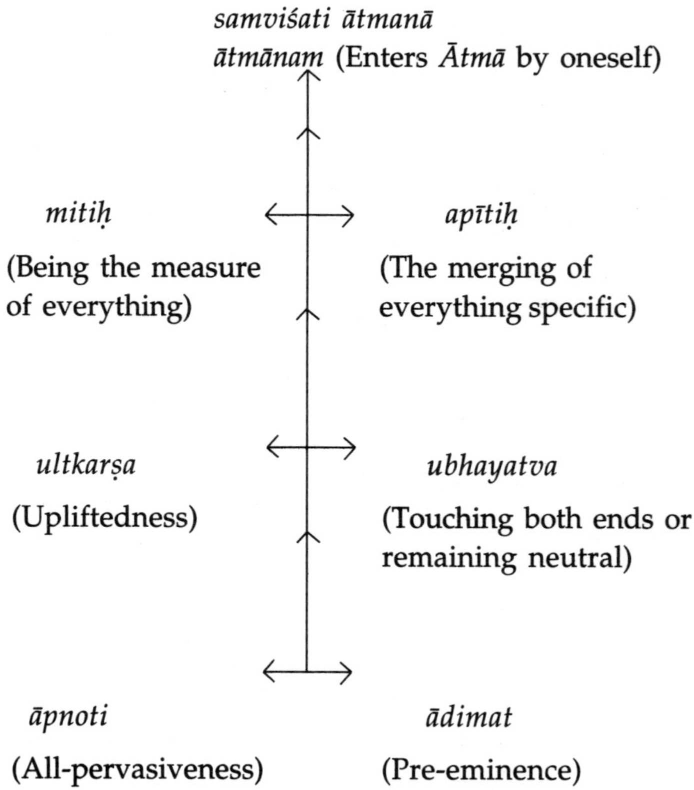

As Existence (*sat*) and Consciousness (*cit*) touch all these four differentiable realms, so too the real, non-dual *ānanda* (Value sense) is to be intuitively perceived as the neutral thread-value that runs vertically through all these levels. It is this one Value-strand that makes all these levels valuable in human life.

Experiencing the neutrality of this non-dual value sense or *ānanda* through equating the four quarters of *Ātmā* with the four constituent elements of the sacred syllable *auṁ*, is the note with which the Upaniṣad ends. The words *"ya evam veda"* (he who knows thus) are repeated twice to mark the end of the text and underscore the purely personal nature of this experience.

AUṀ

शान्तिपाठः (Śāntipāṭhaḥ)

ॐ भद्रं कर्णेभिः शृणुयाम देवा।
भद्रं पश्येमाक्षभिर्यजत्राः।
स्थिरैरंगैस्तुष्टुवाँ सस्तनूभिर्
व्यशेम देवहितं यदायुः॥
स्वस्ति न इन्द्रो वृद्धश्रवाः
स्वस्ति नः पूषा विश्ववेदाः।
स्वस्ति नस्तार्क्ष्यो अरिष्टनेमिः
स्वस्ति नो बृहस्पतिर्दधातु॥
ॐ शान्तिः शान्तिः शान्तिः॥

auṁ bhadraṁ karṇebhiḥ śṛṇuyāma devā ।
bhadram paśyemākṣabhir yajatrāḥ ।
sthirair aṅgais tuṣṭuvāṁ̐ sastanūbhir
vyaśema devahitaṁ yad āyuḥ ॥
svasti na indro vṛddhaśravāḥ
svasti naḥ pūṣā viśvavedāḥ ।

svasti nas tārkṣyo ariṣṭanemiḥ
svasti no bṛhaspatir dadhātu ॥
auṁ śāntiḥ śāntiḥ śāntiḥ ॥

Auṁ. May we, with our ears hear that
Which is auspicious, O gods!
And may we, habitually offering oblations,
See with our eyes that which is auspicious!
With strong bodies, singing your praise,
May we live out our span of life
Destined to us by gods!
May Indra of mature learning
Bestow well-being on us!
May Pūṣā (the Sun) the knower of all,
Bestow well-being on us!

May Tārkṣya (Garuḍa), the annihilator of dangers,
Bestow well-being on us!
May Bṛhaspati bestow well-being on us!
Auṁ Peace! Peace! Peace!

Glossary

Abhidhāna: The name or word that denotes something.

Abhidheya: That which is denoted by an *abhidhāna* (see).

Advaita: Non-duality, transcending every form of duality or multiplicity experienced.

Āgāmī-karma: *Karma*s going to be done in life, in the future (see also *karma*).

Aham brahma asmi: One of the *mahā-vākya*s (see). It means, "I am *Brahman.*"

Ahaṁkāra: The I-sense each individual has.

Ajñāna: Ignorance. The mistaken notion concerning oneself and the world, that what appears manifestly is real, completely oblivious of the one all-underlying Reality called *Brahman* or *Atman* that is indestructible.

Akṣara: That which does not perish. Denotes the eternal Reality. Also means, one of the letters of any alphabet, or a pronounced syllable.

Amṛtam: Immortality or the Immortal Reality. Poetically imagined as the elixir in a golden pot that emerged from the Milk-Ocean, when the *deva*s and the *asura*s churned it together.

Ānanda: Bliss. To be understood as relating to the Good in Western philosophy as a supreme Value. *Sat, cit* and *ānanda* are terms conjointly used to define the Absolute (*Brahman*) in Vedānta. Concerning an individual being, *ānanda* is to be understood as the value consciousness that enables one to evaluate one's own experiences either as pleasant or unpleasant.

Anātmā (Anātman): Non-self. What appears to be real.

Aniṣṭa: The feeling of something being disliked. One of the three attitudes one can have towards any object (see *iṣṭa* and *udāsīna*).

Antaḥkaraṇas: In Indian psychology, the common name for the four mental faculties involved in the process of knowing, namely, *manas* (questioning), *buddhi* (reasoning), *citta* (memorizing and recalling) and *ahaṁkāra* (relating what is known to oneself in terms of value experience).

Asaṁbhūti: The opposite of *saṁbhūti*. Stands for destruction or dissolution in the present Upaniṣad.

Asuras: Demons. The opposite of *suras* or *devas* (gods — the fair or bright entities inhabiting the Vedic heaven). Symbolize those who live dejected with unfulfilled desires.

Ātmā (*Ātman*): The Self (from the root *āt*, meaning "to pervade"). The invisible reality or stuff that pervades all visible forms. Often confused with *jīva*, the soul. Used in a slightly altered sense according to context. The simplest meaning of the word is "I" or "oneself." Also used sometimes to denote one's own body.

Ātma-jñāna: The knowledge of the Self, Self-knowledge, to know oneself.

Ātma-vidyā: Self-knowledge; the science of the Self.

AUṀ: Pronounced "*oṁ*." The most sacred and potential of all words in Indian scriptures. Some consider it even as an object of worship. In Vedic rituals, it is known as *anujñākṣara* (the syllable uttered with which permission is given to begin a ritual) and in the wisdom context of Vedānta, it is the verbal symbol representing *Brahman*, the Absolute. The *Māṇḍūkya Upaniṣad* is solely meant to show how this mono-syllable is so sublime in its meaning.

Avasthā-traya: *Avasthā* — states, *traya* — three. The three alternating states of consciousness, viz., *jāgarita* (waking state), *svapna* (dreaming state) and *suṣupti* (deep sleep).

Avidyā: Nescience or ignorance. The function of consciousness because of which the unreal is taken for the real, and the real for the unreal. The root-cause of illusion and sufferings.

Bhāna: Any apparent manifest form of consciousness. Literally, "lustrous appearance."

Bhāva: Any transient form the eternal Reality (*sat*) assumes. Without *bhāva, sat* never exists, neither can *bhāva*s be there without *sat* existing.

Bhavat: That which happens at present.

Bhaviṣyat: That which happens in future.

Bhoga: Enjoyment derived from objects.

Bhoktā (*Bhoktṛ*): Enjoyer, the subject who enjoys.

Bhoktṛtva: The sense of being the enjoyer (see *bhoga*).

Bhūtam: That which has already come into being.

Brahman: The Absolute. Derived from the verb root *bṛh,* meaning, "to grow constantly." Literally, "that which grows constantly."

Brahma-vidyā: The science of *Brahman* or the Absolute. Another name for Vedānta.

Brahmavit: The knower of *Brahman.*

Buddhi: Understanding. Also denotes the reasoning faculty of mind (see *antaḥkaraṇa*s).

Caturtha: Literally, "the fourth." Denotes the transcendental state of consciousness, also known as *turīya* (see).

Cit: Literally, "Consciousness." The essential content of the imperishable Reality pervading all the perishable and visible forms, is pure Consciouness. Hence, *Brahman* is designated as *cit* in essence. See *sat* and *ānanda* also.

Citta: The memorizing and recalling faculty of mind. One of the *antaḥkaraṇa*s (see).

*Deva*s: Gods. Inhabitants of the Vedic heaven.

Dhana: Wealth.

Dharma: Derived from the root *dhṛ* meaning "to support." The universal functional system that sustains the world and life. Righteous way of life in full harmony with the universal order.

Dhīra: Brave, bold, courageous. Etymologically, "one who imparts knowledge."

Idam sarvam: Everything here. Denotes all the apparent worlds together.

Indriyas: Sense organs. The five sense organs and the five organs of action (speech, hands, feet, excretory organ, genitals) together.

Īśa: The Sanskrit equivalent to God. Literally, "one who controls." It denotes the principle that controls the integral law that sustains each entity as a particular mode of expression of the universal being.

Iṣṭa: That which is liked and felt favourable. Its opposite is *aniṣṭa.*

Īśvara: Īśa+vara. The Sanskrit equivalent to God. *Īśa,* literally, the one who controls everything; *vara,* means the highest.

Jagat: The world. Literally, that which is always on the move.

Jāgrat: The waking state (*jāgarita*) of consciousness.

Jñāna: Wisdom. In the Vedāntic context, the Wisdom of the non-difference of oneself from the universal Reality. The way of *jñāna* (*jñāna-mārga*) is contrasted with that of rituals and actions (*karma-mārga*).

Jñāna-kāṇḍa: The sections of the Vedic texts that purely deals with Wisdom (*jñāna*).

Jñāna-yoga: The *yoga* state attained through *jñāna* (see). The state of experiencing one's own oneness with the all-underlying Reality with Wisdom (*jñāna*) as a means.

Jñānendriyas: The five senses of knowledge.

Jñānin: One who possesses *jñāna* (see).

Jñātā (*jñātṛ*)*:* The knower, the subject in contrast to the object (*jñeya*).

Jñātṛtva: One's sense of being the knower.

Kāraṇa-śarīra: The body with which happiness is unconsciously experienced in deep sleep.

Karma: All actions in general. Philosophically, the creative urge inherent in the imperishable Reality, causing the emergence of all manifest forms from Itself. In the Vedic context, the ritual of burnt-sacrifice enjoined by the Vedas. As a religious belief of the Hindus, the incipient memory factors clinging to the souls as a result of their past deeds. All are bound to enjoy or suffer the fruits of their deeds, and will have to be reborn for this purpose. One might accumulate more *karmas* in the next birth. This vicious chain of action goes on until one attains final release. Such *karmas* are divided into three categories — *sañcita-karmas* (the actions accumulated in all previous births), *āgāmī-karmas* (fresh actions yet to be done in the present life-span) and *prārabdha karmas* (actions already initiated but eating of their fruits is not finished with).

Karma-bandha: The bondage caused by one's sense of being the doer of *karmas* (see).

Karma-kāṇḍa: The section of the Vedic texts that deals with rituals, consisting of hymns praising various deities, and detailed instructions on how to perform *yajñas*.

Karma-yoga: The *yoga* of action. Realizing one's oneness with the total existence by means of performing deeds with the awareness that all actions belong to total nature, not to any individual being.

Karmendriyas: The organs of action *vāk* (speech), *pāṇi* (hands), *pāda* (feet), *pāyu* (excretory organ), *upastha* (genitals).

Kartā: The doer of *karmas*, the agency of action.

Kartṛtva: One's sense of being the doer of *karmas* (see).

Kīrti: Fame. One of the worldly values cherished by all.

Kṛtam: That which is done; that which is created.

Kṣara: That which perishes. Refers to the apparent world.

Lakṣaṇa: Definition. The distinguishing marks of something.

Lakṣaṇārtha: Indirect meaning of a sentence.

Mahā-bhūtas: The five basic elements that constitute the world, namely, *ākāśa* (space), *vāyu* (air), *agni* or *tejas* (fire) *ap* or *jala* (water), *pṛthivī* or *bhūmi* (earth).

Mahā-vākyas: Literally, "the great dicta." The conclusive formulae of Vedāntic Wisdom, such as *tat tvam asi* (That thou art), *aham brahmāsmi* (I am *Brahman*), *prajñānam brahma* (*Brahman* is Consciousness), *ayam ātmā brahma* (this self is *Brahman*), *auṁ tat sat* (*auṁ*, that is what is Real), *sarvam khalvidam brahma* (everything here indeed is *Brahman*).

Manana: Intense cogitation on what is directly heard from the *guru* (*śravaṇa*), leading finally to full conviction and realization (*nididhyāsana*).

Manas: Mind. *Manas* consists of the questioning and imagining faculties of consciousness. That which is constituted of *manas* is called *manomaya.*

Manīṣin: A wise person.

Mantra: A Vedic hymn or sacred prayer. The portion of Vedas including the Saṁhitās, distinguished from Brāhmaṇas and Upaniṣads.

Mātrā: A measure. A unit of measure. In the *Māṇḍūkya Upaniṣad,* each letter of *AUṀ* is counted as a *mātrā* that stands for a *pāda* (quarter) of the function of conciousness.

Māyā: The mysterious urge inherent in the Absolute (*Brahman* or *Ātman*) to unfold itself as all the worlds and the phenomenon of life. The very appearing of the world caused thus ends up in becoming a sort of veil put over the Absolute hiding its vision from our view and making the illusory vision that the apparent world is the real.

Moha: Confused or deluded state of mind.

Mṛtyu: Death.

Mukti (Mokṣa): Final liberation. Literally, "freedom." Signifies the freedom from all bondages.

Mūlā-tiraskaraṇī: Literally, "the casual veil." Denotes the state in which everything remains hidden in a causal Darkness.

Nāma: Name. *Nāma* along with *rūpa* (form) distinguishes every individual entity from others in this world.

Nivṛtti-mārga: The way of withdrawal, followed by those who are interested in Wisdom. See *pravṛtti-mārga.*

Pāda: Quarter, foot.

Pāpa: Sin.

Paramānanda: Supreme Happiness. (See *Ānanda*)

Pāramārthika: This is contrasted with *vyāvahārika*. Relating to the ultimate metaphysical Reality (*paramārtha*) — *Parama,* ultimate; and *artha,* the meaning content.

Phalaśruti: The envoy at the end of the text or of the chapters of scriptures; clarifying the benefit of acquiring the wisdom taught therein.

Prājña: Name denoting the consciousness during deep sleep state.

Prajñānam brahma: One of the *mahā-vākyas* (great dicta) of Vedānta. It means, "*Brahman* is Consciousness."

Prajāpati: Literally, "the Lord of those who are born." Name applied to the Creator as the progenitor of all living beings, and represents an ontological version of Brahmā the Creator.

Prakaraṇa-grantha: Introductory textbook on any subject.

Prakṛti: Nature. Literally, "that which is always in an active state." This activeness is inherent in the ultimate Reality or *Brahman*. *Brahman* in its active state is called *prakṛti*.

Prāṇa: The vital breath. The functions of vital breath are identified as five, namely *prāṇa* (going upward), *apāna* (going downward), *vyāna* (that which takes vitality to every part of the body), *samāna* (that which keeps the balance of the body), and *udāna* (that which leaves the body at death).

Praṇava: Another word for *AUṀ*. Literally "the ever new."

Prārabdha-karma: See *karma*.

Prasthāna-traya: The three basic source books of Vedānta, namely, the Upaniṣads, *Bhagavad Gītā* and *Brahma-sūtras*.

Pravivikta-bhuk: The state of enjoying in loneliness. A distinguishing mark of the function of consciousness in the dreaming state.

Pravṛtti-mārga: The way of active involvement, as against *nivṛtti-mārga* (see) followed by those who are interested in rituals and actions.

Puṇya: Merit as against *pāpa* (sin).

Puruṣa: Literally, "person." The word is used both in universal and particular senses, In the universal sense, He is the cosmic person who has the entire cosmos for his body. In this sense He is ofter called *virāṭ puruṣa*. In the particular sense, the word denotes the individuated consciousness that possesses each body.

Pūṣā: An epithet of Sun-god.

Rūpa: Form. Along with *nāma* (name), it distinguishes every individual entity from others in this world. Hence the world is often spoken of as constituted of *nāmas* and *rūpas*.

Sādhanā: A spiritual discipline undergone for the attainment of a particular goal (*sidhhi*).

Samāna: One of the five functional subdivisions of *prāṇa.* Its function is to equalize the distribution of vitality and thus maintain the balanced state of the organism.

Samaṣṭi: The universal (see *vyaṣṭi).*

Saṁbhūti: Becoming. Any emergence of a new form as part of the creative unfoldment of *Brahman.*

Saṁhitā: Literally, "that which is conjoined inseparably." Name of the initial part of the Vedas, dealing mainly with rituals. Also called *mantra* (see).

Saṁkalpa: Mind's wilful imagining.

Samvit: Another word for *cit*. Pure Consciousness.

Śānti-pāṭha: Peace Invocation.

Sañcita-karma: See *karma.*

Sarvam: Everything. Stands for all the worlds together.

Sarveśvara: Sarva+īśvara. The controller of everything.

Sat: That which always exists. The subsisting Reality in all the transistory forms of the visible world, even as gold is the subsisting reality in all ornaments. *Brahman,* as this subsisting Reality, is designated as *sat.* (See *ānanda* and *cit* also.)

Sat-cit-ānanda (saccidānanda): Existence-Consciousness Value experience; the only positive definition of *Brahman*. (See *sat, cit* and *ānanda* also).

Satya-dharma: A person in whom the awareness of Reality (*satya*) and righteousness in life (*dharma*) fuse together and become one.

So'ham: One of the famous dicta in Vedānta, meaning, "He is myself."

Sthūla: That which is gross.

Sthūla-bhāna: The gross manifestation of Consciousness, the ultimate Reality, resulting in the experience of the gross (*sthūla*) world.

Sthūla-saṁkalpanā: The gross wilful imagination of Consciousness that results in the appearance of the gross world.

Sthūla-śarīra: The gross body with the help of which consciousness in its waking state becomes aware of the gross world.

Sūkta: Literally "good saying." Signifies each of the Vedic hymns.

Sūkṣma-śarīra: The subtle body with the help of which consciousness creates and enjoys dreams.

Suras: Gods, inhabitants of heaven, literally, "those who give abundantly."

Sūrya: The Sun.

Suṣupti: Deep sleep.

Svayambhū: That which is self-created; that which exists on its own. Signifies *Brahman*.

Svapna: Literally, the sleeping state. As a functional state of consciousness, it denotes the dreaming state.

Taijasa: Name denoting consciousness during the dreaming state.

Tanmātrā: Tat (that) + *mātrā* (mere). The thing in itself.

Tāpa-traya: Three kinds of sufferings — *ādhyātmika* (self-created), *ādhibhautika* (those caused by others or other beings), *ādhidaivika* (caused by fate).

Tat-tvam-asi: "That thou art," one of the *mahā-vākyas* (see).

Trikālātīta: Beyond the past, present and future. The timeless.

Tripuṭi: The three factors of all knowing situations: The knower, the known and knowledge.

Turīya: Literally, "the fourth." The transcendental state of consciousness in which the *tripuṭi* (see) merges in the all engulfing Self-radiance. Narayana Guru defines it as, "To know transparently that which is bottomless and topless, from top to bottom."

Turīya-bhāna: The mode of consciousness in which one is fully aware, "I am *Brahman* indeed."

Udāsīna: Indifference; the state in which no like or dislike persists.

Vācyārtha: Literal sense of a word or sentence.

Vaiśvānara: The *Ātmā* conceived as the vital force that keeps the entire cosmic system alive. In the *Māṇḍūkya Upaniṣad,* it denotes the functional state of consciousness during the waking state.

Vānaprastha: The third stage of human life, in which one leaves household affairs to one's children and proceeds to forest areas for leading a contemplative life.

Vedānta: Literally, "the end part of the Vedas," as referring to the Upaniṣads. Also means the end of knowledge, signifying the philosophy of the Upaniṣads, because the Wisdom it teaches puts an end to one's quest for knowledge.

Vedas: The earliest of the Indian scriptures, collected into four volumes, namely, the *Ṛgveda, Yajurveda, Sāmaveda,* and *Atharvaveda.* They praise Indra, Varuṇa, Mitra and other phenomenal gods of nature. The word literally means "knowledge."

Vidyā: Knowledge or science. That function of consciousness because of which one understands the Real as the real and the unreal as the unreal.

Vijñāna: Any specific or applied form of knowledge or Wisdom.

Vināśa: Destruction, dissolution. Also termed *asaṁbhūti* in the *Īśa Upaniṣad.*

Viṣayas: Any object of knowledge.

Viveka: Discrimination. The natural capability in one to discriminate the eternal from the transient in life, both existence-wise and value-wise.

Vyaṣṭi: The particular (see *samaṣṭi*).

Vyāvahārika: That which is related to the day to day affairs of life, in contrast to *pāramārthika* (see).

Yajña: Sacrifice. The Vedic fire-sacrifice. It denotes offering what is considered as possessed by an individual back to the universal *prakṛti* to which everything, including ourselves really belongs.

Yama: To restrain. The first step of the spiritual practice according to Patañjali's Yoga system; it consists of *ahiṁsā* (non-hurting), *satyam* (speaking truth), *asteya* (non-stealing), *brahmacarya* (continence), *aparigraha* (non-acquisitiveness) — all body-based disciplines. Also the name of the god of death.

Yoga: (From the root *yuj* meaning, joining together). Each finding their inseparable oneness with the one causal Reality, just as an ornament finds its oneness with gold.

As a contemplative method of self-enquiry, the way of expressing an inexpressible reality by showing its two opposite expressible sides and leaving the unitive meaning to be intuitively perceived by the reader or seeker on his own. For example, attaining immortality and crossing over death are two expressions that mean the same. But these two expressions are opposite in nature. They have in between them a meaning that cannot be expressed as it is.

Different systems of *yoga* have been developed in India, each giving emphasis to some particular pair to be joined together. Patañjali's system is known as *Rāja-Yoga.* The names such as *Haṭha-Yoga, Karma-Yoga, Jñāna-Yoga, Bhakti-Yoga* are popular. Each of the eighteen chapters of the *Bhagavad Gītā* is also named a *yoga.* The *Bhagvad Gītā* claims itself to be a *Yoga-Śāstra* (textbook on the science of *yoga*).

Yoga-buddhi: The awareness attained by the method of *yoga* (see *Yoga*).

Yoga-Śāstra: The science of *Yoga.* A method of scientific thinking, equivalent to dialectics as conceived by Plato. The *Bhagavad Gītā* claims itself to be a *Yoga-śāstra.* (See *Yoga*).

Yoni: Literally, the genital organ of a woman. Philosophically, the source of everything.

Index